HARD QUESTIONS
Prophetic Answers

HARD QUESTIONS
Prophetic Answers

DOCTRINAL PERSPECTIVES ON DIFFICULT CONTEMPORARY ISSUES

Daniel K Judd

DESERET
BOOK

Salt Lake City, Utah

Library of Congress Cataloging-in-Publication Data

Judd, Daniel K
  Hard questions, prophetic answers / Daniel K Judd.
      p.   cm.
Includes bibliographical references and index.
  ISBN 1-59038-225-0 (pbk.)
  1. Church of Jesus Christ of Latter-day Saints—
Doctrines—Miscellanea. 2. Christian ethics—Mormon
authors—Miscellanea.   I. Title.
BX8635.3.J84 2004
230'.9332—dc22
                                                    2003026590

Printed in the United States of America   18961-7171
R. R. Donnelley and Sons, Crawfordsville, IN

10   9   8   7   6   5   4   3   2   1

To my wife and friend, Kaye Seegmiller Judd

Contents

Acknowledgments

First and foremost, I express appreciation to my wife, Kaye, for her support and encouragement throughout the completion of this project. I also want to acknowledge the support and sacrifice of my remarkable children, Jake, Jessi, Rachel, and Adam. My parents, LeRoy and Phyllis Judd, though their assignments in mortality are nearing an honorable end, continue to be a source of great strength.

Special thanks to the faculty, administration, and staff of the Department of Ancient Scripture in Religious Education at Brigham Young University. My secretary, Holly Rogers, and research assistant, Ben Rogers, have shown remarkable skill and great support. Thanks also to Rachel Clark, Laura Webb, Becky McCarty, Emily Cram, and JaLee Clarke for their secretarial assistance. The support, encouragement, and professional skills of Cory Maxwell, Suzanne Brady, Sheryl Smith, Tonya Facemyer, Laurie Cook, and others at Deseret Book have also been an important part of this project.

Finally, I want to express my sincere appreciation to the many people who are faithful in their struggle to answer the difficult questions in their lives. I find great strength in observing and sometimes being a part of the lives of those who, in spite of great opposition, continue faithful and valiant in their testimonies of Jesus Christ and the restoration of His gospel.

I have endeavored to be true to the words and teachings of Jesus Christ as well as to the prophets, both ancient and modern, but this book is my own interpretation and application of what they have taught. This publication does not in any way officially represent The Church of Jesus Christ of Latter-day Saints or Brigham Young University.

Introduction

The restoration of The Church of Jesus Christ began with a young boy seeking answers to difficult questions. In addition to wanting to know "which of all the sects was right" (Joseph Smith–History 1:18), young Joseph Smith Jr. had other serious questions on his mind as well. Elder Henry B. Eyring said: "From studying the various accounts of the First Vision, we learn that young Joseph went into the grove not only to learn which church he should join but also to obtain forgiveness for his sins—something he seems not to have understood how to do."[1]

Joseph's heartfelt questions concerning church affiliation, personal worthiness, and numerous other doctrinal, procedural, and personal matters during the years that followed led eventually to the reestablishment of the Savior's Church and the restoration of the "most plain and precious parts of the gospel of the Lamb" (1 Nephi 13:34), which had been lost from the earth since the days of Jesus Christ and His apostles. The mortal ministry of the Prophet Joseph Smith began and ended well over a century ago, but his method of seeking divine direction concerning the difficult questions he faced is an important example to us still.

This book deals with several "hard questions" (1 Kings 10:1) faced by Latter-day Saints today. Some of the questions are timeless; others are unique to our particular time. The questions addressed here, as well as other questions we may be pondering, may not have the same historical significance as the questions asked by the Prophet Joseph. Nonetheless, they are vitally important to us, to the Lord, and to those with whom we have influence. There are some difficult questions for which answers have not been revealed (Alma 37:11), but many, perhaps even most, can be answered if we are faithful and diligent in our search as well as willing to accept responsibility for the consequences of knowing the answers. Elder Neal A. Maxwell teaches that hard questions are usually associated with hard doctrines:

> When one decides whether or not to deal with hard doctrines, the tendency is to put them off or to be put off by them. Not only are they in some respects puzzling, but they may even offend our mortal pride. Just as there are some good deeds we do gladly and quickly (while others are put off time and again), so it is with certain gospel truths: we accept some with joy and alacrity [promptness], but others we keep at arm's length. The hardness is

usually not in their complexity, but in the deep demands these doctrines make of us.[2]

The issues dealt with here and the questions and doctrinal answers associated with them are stumbling blocks for some and stepping-stones for others in their own spiritual and intellectual journeys. Some answers will be in direct opposition to the wisdom of the world. They may be considered foolishness by some and profound by others. The apostle Paul wrote: "But the natural man receiveth not the things of the Spirit of God: for they are foolishness unto him: neither can he know them, because they are spiritually discerned" (1 Corinthians 2:14). President Harold B. Lee explained that our only promise of safety is to follow the counsel of our prophets, seers, and revelators:

> Now the only safety we have as members of this church is to do exactly what the Lord said to the Church in that day when the Church was organized. We must learn to give heed to the words and commandments that the Lord shall give through his prophet, "as he receiveth them, walking in all holiness before me; . . . as if from mine own mouth, in all patience and faith." (D&C 21:4–5.) There will be some things that take patience and faith. You may not like what comes from the authority of the Church. It may contradict your political views. It may contradict your social views. It may interfere with some of your social life. But if you listen to these things, as if from the mouth of the Lord himself, with patience and

3

faith, the promise is that "the gates of hell shall not prevail against you; yea, and the Lord God will disperse the powers of darkness from before you, and cause the heavens to shake for your good, and his name's glory." (D&C 21:6)[3]

Even though many answers to the questions in this volume contradict worldly philosophies, I have taken great care to avoid a contentious spirit. The Savior and His servants have taught that "the spirit of contention is not of me, but is of the devil" (3 Nephi 11:29) and our "criticism may be worse than the conduct [we] are trying to correct."[4]

The phrase "hard questions" is taken from the biblical account of an interchange between King Solomon and the queen of Sheba during her visit to ancient Israel: "When the queen of Sheba heard of the fame of Solomon concerning the name of the Lord, she came to prove him with *hard questions*" (1 Kings 10:1; emphasis added). After meeting with Solomon, the queen responded to his inspired counsel, "I believed not the words, until I came, and mine eyes had seen it: and, behold, the half was not told me: thy wisdom and prosperity exceedeth the fame which I heard" (1 Kings 10:7).

Just as the Lord provided counsel to His people anciently, so has He given us the privilege to receive direction today from prophets, seers, revelators, and other inspired leaders and teachers. The answers to the difficult questions addressed in this book have been taken primarily from the teachings of prophets, both ancient and modern. Relevant research findings have also been included as a kind of second witness to their inspired counsel.

One underlying theme throughout is the warning from our leaders that we as a people, in some cases, are allowing the philosophies of the world to eclipse the doctrines of God as taught in scripture and in the counsel of living prophets. President Joseph F. Smith stated:

> The tendency has been, during all these years, to get farther away from the principles of the gospel as they are contained in the holy scriptures. The worship of reason, of false philosophy, is greater now than it was then. Men are depending upon their own research to find out God, and that which they cannot discover and which they can not demonstrate to their satisfaction through their own research and their natural senses, they reject. They arc not seeking for the Spirit of the Lord, they are not striving to know God in the manner in which he has marked out by which he may be known, but they are walking in their own way, believing in their own man-made philosophies, and teaching the doctrines of devils and not the doctrines of the Son of God.[5]

This statement, given by President Smith during general conference in 1917, is strikingly descriptive of the relationship of the doctrines of God and the philosophies of men today. It is also consistent with King Mosiah's warning in the Book of Mormon: "If the time comes that the voice of the people doth choose iniquity, then is the time that the judgments of God will come upon you; yea, then is the time he will visit you with great destruction even as he has hitherto visited this land" (Mosiah 29:27; see also Helaman 5:2).

It is important to consider what "the voice of the people" is today. Where are our opinions concerning the vital issues of the day? What do we believe about how we should balance our time? What about marriage and divorce? War? Depression? Same-sex attraction? Anger? Abuse? Are our beliefs and practices in harmony with the teachings of scripture and our living prophets, or are our beliefs more consistent with the philosophies of the world?

In addition to learning from the teachings and warnings of prophets, it is important to note that we may also find truth in places other than scripture and prophetic counsel. President Brigham Young stated: "Every art and science known and studied by the children of men is comprised within the Gospel."[6] There are indeed some precepts of men that have been given through inspiration. The prophet Nephi taught, "Cursed is he that putteth his trust in man, or maketh flesh his arm, or shall hearken unto the precepts of men, save their precepts shall be given by the power of the Holy Ghost" (2 Nephi 28:31). President Hugh B. Brown counseled:

> The Church of Jesus Christ of Latter-day Saints accepts newly revealed truth, whether it comes through direct revelation or from study and research. We deny the common conception of reality that distinguishes radically between the natural and the supernatural, between the

temporal and the eternal, between the sacred and the secular. For us, there is no order of reality that is utterly different in character from the world of which we are a part, that is separated from us by an impassable gulf. We do not separate our daily mundane tasks and interests from the meaning and substance of religion. We recognize the spiritual in all phases and aspects of living and realize that this life is an important part of eternal life. We aspire to the best of which we are intrinsically capable and will think our thoughts, fashion our ideals, and pursue every task firm in the faith that in a very real sense we are living in the presence of God here and now.[7]

Nonetheless, truth gleaned from study and research is not the focus of the answers provided in this book. Rather, I have attempted to emphasize the transcendence of scripture and doctrine while acknowledging the proper place that science, academic, and clinical research have in Latter-day Saint theology and practice.

Each chapter addresses a specific topic and related questions of concern, followed by a discussion of the doctrinal principles and appropriate research findings that address the related questions. Working with many individuals and families over the years who have voiced these and similar questions has given me the opportunity to consider what the apostle Peter described as the "reason of the hope that is in [me]" (1 Peter 3:15). As I interact with my own family, members of my stake, students and colleagues at Brigham Young University, friends, acquaintances, and scholars from around the world, I am constantly humbled to recognize how blessed we are as Latter-day Saints to have the restored gospel as revealed through the Prophet Joseph Smith and succeeding prophets. I have endeavored to be true to the teachings of scripture and the words of living prophets, but this work is my own and is not intended to be an official representation of The Church of Jesus Christ of Latter-day Saints nor of Brigham Young University.

Along with the teachings of latter-day apostles and the scriptures, which are given highest priority in addressing the various issues raised here, another source of truth should be given priority as well—the direction of the Holy Ghost. If you have a particular issue of special interest, remember that our Heavenly Father guides us through the influence of His Spirit. As important as doctrinal discussions, intellectual reasoning, and even physical proofs may be, they are secondary to "the evidence of things not seen" (Hebrews 11:1).

After describing several experiences in which he had been privileged to hear logical arguments and even behold angelic manifestations in answer to his questions, President Wilford Woodruff testified concerning the transcendence of the testimony borne of the Holy Ghost:

> Now, I have had all these testimonies, and they are true. But with all these, I have never had any testimony since I have been in the flesh, that has been greater than the testimony of the Holy Ghost. That is the strongest testimony that can be given to me or to any man in the

flesh. Now, every man has a right to that, and when he obtains it, it is a living witness to him. It deceives no man, and never has. Lucifer may appear to man in the capacity of an angel of light; but there is no deception with the Holy Ghost.[8]

The prophet Nephi counseled:

> Wherefore, now after I have spoken these words, if ye cannot understand them it will be because ye ask not, neither do ye knock; wherefore, ye are not brought into the light, but must perish in the dark.
>
> For behold, again I say unto you that if ye will enter in by the way, and receive the Holy Ghost, it will show unto you all things what ye should do. (2 Nephi 32:4–5)

Such counsel to rely on the guidance of the Holy Ghost comes with an important caution. The Prophet Joseph Smith taught that "nothing is a greater injury to the children of men than to be under the influence of a false spirit when they think they have the Spirit of God."[9] Perhaps that is one reason why the Lord provides direction in our minds as well as in our hearts: "Behold, I will tell you in your mind and in your heart, by the Holy Ghost, which shall come upon you and which shall dwell in your heart" (D&C 8:2).

Even though we are living in what President Gordon B. Hinckley describes as "the greatest season in the history of the Church," our prophets and apostles have also warned us that the "perilous times" (2 Timothy 3:1) described by the apostle

Paul are "now upon us."[10] Never has the Church been larger, stronger, or more able, but never have such a variety and complexity of problems and questions been before us. President Harold B. Lee warned:

> We have some tight places to go before the Lord is through with this church and the world in this dispensation, which is the last dispensation, which shall usher in the coming of the Lord. The gospel was restored to prepare a people ready to receive him. The power of Satan will increase; we see it in evidence on every hand. There will be inroads within the Church . . . We will see those who profess membership but secretly are plotting and trying to lead people not to follow the leadership that the Lord has set up to preside in this church.[11]

Many of these "tight places" we face may come as questions concerning the doctrines, policies, and practices of the Church. The kinds of questions we ask, the spirit in which we ask them, the answers we receive, and the source from which we receive those answers can have tremendous influence on our making it through the difficult times we face now as well as those difficult times yet to come.

As I have attempted to follow the apostle Paul's counsel to avoid "foolish and unlearned questions . . . knowing that they do gender strifes" (2 Timothy 2:23), I have learned that carefully listening to difficult questions and addressing them can bring significant opportunities for growth. The Prophet Joseph Smith stated, "By proving contraries, truth is made manifest."[12]

I have come to understand why the heart of Ammon, the great missionary among the Lamanites, swelled "with joy" (Alma 17:29) when he and the other servants of King Lamoni were confronted by a greedy and angry mob as they watered King Lamoni's flocks. The other servants feared for their lives, but Ammon saw the situation as an opportunity to "show forth my power unto these my fellow-servants, or the power which is in me, in restoring these flocks unto the king, that I may win the hearts of these my fellow-servants, that I may lead them to believe in my words" (Alma 17:29).

Ammon viewed his greatest challenges as opportunities to learn, refine his understanding, and teach the gospel of Christ to all who would listen. The apostle Paul may have been teaching the same principle to the Saints at Corinth when he stated: "For first of all, when ye come together in the church, I hear that there be divisions among you; and I partly believe it. For *there must be also heresies among you,* that they which are approved may be made manifest among you" (1 Corinthians 11:18–19; emphasis added). Though most of us have not faced the physical challenges faced by Ammon at the waters of Sebus, many of us have faced and will yet face doctrinal differences and cultural challenges such as those confronted by the apostle Paul at Corinth. Discussing such differences can sometimes be unsettling, but if we approach these discussions with humility, with a firm understanding of the gospel, and by "speaking the truth in love" (Ephesians 4:15), much good can be done and much truth can be learned.

The gospel of Jesus Christ provides answers to the most

pressing problems burdening the world. The "great question" underlying each of the issues addressed here is the question Amulek spoke of as he taught the once-faithful Zoramites: "We have beheld that the great question which is in your minds is whether the word be in the Son of God, or whether there shall be no Christ" (Alma 34:5). It is my sincere hope that this book will assist you in the great cause in which we are engaged—to "come unto Christ" (Moroni 10:30).

CHAPTER ONE

Self, Family, Church, Profession:

How Can a Proper Balance Be Achieved?

In a worldwide satellite broadcast to Church leaders, President Gordon B. Hinckley spoke of balancing the many demands placed upon them and upon their families: "I have been where many of you are today. Let me say that there is never enough time to do it all." While acknowledging the great challenge it is to balance the varied dimensions of life, President Hinckley reminded those listening of the importance of meeting their responsibilities to family, profession, and Church, and to caring for themselves. He provided two important suggestions for balancing busy lives: "There is only one way you can get it all done. That is to follow the direction which the Lord gave Joseph Smith. To him He said: 'organize yourselves; prepare every needful thing'" (D&C 88:119).

President Hinckley added: "The Lord does not expect us to be supermen. But if we will place ourselves in His hands, if we will plead with Him in prayer, He will inspire us and help us. He will magnify us and make us equal to the responsibility."[1] The prophet's counsel to place ourselves in the Lord's hands is the most important and effective key in helping us to balance the many challenges and demands of our lives.

THE CHALLENGE OF DISTRACTION

"Trust in the Lord with all thine heart; and lean not unto thine own understanding. In all thy ways acknowledge him, and he shall direct thy paths" (Proverbs 3:5–6). These familiar and yet profound verses of scripture recorded thousands of years ago provide an ancient witness to latter-day counsel concerning the timeless standard by which we should direct our lives. Could difficulty in balancing our lives result from confusion about what it means to place our trust in God and to follow His direction? Elder Richard G. Scott of the Quorum of the Twelve Apostles asked a similar question:

> Are there so many fascinating, exciting things to do or so many challenges pressing down upon you that it is hard to keep focused on that which is essential? When things of the world crowd in, all too often the wrong things take highest priority. Then it is easy to forget the fundamental purpose of life. Satan has a powerful tool to use against good people. It is distraction. He would have good people fill life with "good things" so there is no room for the essential ones. Have you unconsciously been caught in that trap?[2]

As Elder Scott suggests, distraction can come in many

forms. Sometimes our attempts to include and balance so many good things in our lives leave us too little time, too little energy, and too few resources to focus on how the Lord would have us live our lives. As we juggle our personal, professional, and civic responsibilities, how many of us have felt guilt, frustration, and sometimes even irritation when we hear yet another sacrament meeting talk, Relief Society lesson, or quorum instruction on the importance of doing one thing or another that is not a regular part of our lives? How often do we find that the day has passed and we have not offered a meaningful prayer or spent time reading scripture or really connected with our spouse or children? Or that the month has passed and we have not taken the time to attend the temple or complete our home or visiting teaching assignments? Do our young people see attendance at their Church activities as an inconvenience and as a second choice when they are also invited to participate in competing school or community activities? What about our own attendance at Church meetings, the responsibilities associated with our formal Church callings, welfare projects, Young Women's and Scout camp? Or the financial contributions we are sometimes asked to make in addition to our tithes and offerings? Isn't the heart of the problem the sheer number of Church activities and responsibilities we are asked to be involved in? Isn't the answer for us to pick and choose which Church programs we feel are best and drop out of the rest? Shouldn't we be more assertive and simply tell the bishop no when he or one of his counselors asks us to do something in the Church we feel would disrupt our lives?

Better yet, couldn't the First Presidency simply drop some of the many Church programs and by so doing help to reduce the demands placed upon us?

Many churches have lessened the demands placed upon their membership so dramatically that sacrifice is no longer a part of their faith. Although the following invitation was obviously intended by its author to be humorous, it illustrates what some church members are demanding and what some churches are offering:

> Has the heaviness of your old-fashioned church got you weighted down? Try us! We are the New and Improved Lite Church of the Valley. Studies have shown we have 24% fewer commitments than other churches. We guarantee to trim off guilt, because we are Low-Cal . . . low Calvin, that is. We are the home of the 7.5% tithe. We promise 35 minute worship services, with 7 minute sermons. Next Sunday's exciting text is the story of the Feeding of the 500.
>
> We have only 6 Commandments—Your choice!! We use just 3 gospels in our contemporary New Testament, "Good Sound Bites for Modern Human Beings." We take the offering every other week, all major credit cards accepted, of course. We are looking forward with great anticipation to our 800 year Millennium.
>
> Yes, the New and Improved Lite Church of the Valley could be just what you are looking for. We are everything you want in a church . . . and less!![3]

Though the First Presidency recognizes the increased complexity of the times in which we are living and is doing much to "reduce and simplify activities whenever possible,"[4] the reality is that as Latter-day Saints we are always going to have more to do than time will allow, and we will often be asked to make sacrifices as we do our part in building the kingdom of God. The Prophet Joseph Smith observed:

> A religion that does not require the sacrifice of all things never has power sufficient to produce the faith necessary unto life and salvation; for, from the first existence of man, the faith necessary unto the enjoyment of life and salvation never could be obtained without the sacrifice of all earthly things.[5]

The day that sacrifice is no longer a part of our lives will be the day we lose our connection with the Savior and the legacy left to us by the many faithful Saints of the past upon whose shoulders we stand today.

The answers we are seeking about how we can better balance our difficult and often complex lives are actually more about what we include rather than what we exclude from our lives. President Ezra Taft Benson provided an important key to help us decide how to order our lives and where and how to spend our time:

> When we put God first, all other things fall into their proper place or drop out of our lives. Our love of the Lord will govern the claims for our affection, the

demands on our time, the interests we pursue, and the order of our priorities. We should put God ahead of *everyone else* in our lives.[6]

The Prophet Joseph Smith taught, "Such was and always will be, the situation of the saints of God, that unless they have an actual knowledge that the course they are pursuing is according to the will of God they will grow weary in their minds and faint."[7] Even though the specific answers to our many questions about balancing our lives may not always be obvious, prophets both ancient and modern have identified the path that will eventually lead us to the correct answers we are seeking—as well as the correct questions we should be asking.

The Savior taught His ancient apostles, "But seek ye first the kingdom of God, and his righteousness; and all these things shall be added unto you" (Matthew 6:33). Jesus gave a similar answer to the Pharisee who asked, "Master, which is the great commandment in the law? Jesus said unto him, Thou shalt love the Lord thy God with all thy heart, and with all thy soul, and with all thy mind. This is the first and great commandment. And the second is like unto it, Thou shalt love thy neighbour as thyself" (Matthew 22:36–39). Some have argued that the wording of this particular text also implies that we should love *ourselves* as well as our *neighbor* and *God*. Though this reference to *self* is probably best understood in terms of the Golden Rule—"whatsoever ye would that men should do to you, do ye even so to them" (Matthew 7:12; 3 Nephi 14:12)— it is clear that we are going contrary to God's counsel when we reverse, distort, or neglect the divine priority of love of God followed by love of neighbor. This loss of balance occurs when we focus on our own lives to the exclusion of God and neighbor.

SCRIPTURAL ACCOUNTS OF PUTTING FIRST THINGS FIRST

The scriptures contain numerous accounts of men, women, and nations who struggled to understand what it meant to conduct their lives in the way God would have them live. Achieving balance and maintaining the right priorities were a struggle for those people anciently, just as they are for us today. The following are two accounts of faithful people who allowed good things to get in the way of better things and thus experienced the anxiety and exhaustion that go with confused priorities.

Moses

"And it came to pass . . . that Moses sat to judge the people: and the people stood by Moses from the morning unto the evening" (Exodus 18:13). Moses, like many well-meaning Church leaders (and perhaps parents as well), felt it was his responsibility always to be available and to give the people all of the time they requested in solving their personal and family problems. Jethro, Moses' father-in-law, saw what Moses was attempting to do and asked him a question that all who are involved in Church service and in rearing a family need to ask: "What is this thing that thou doest to the people? why sittest thou thyself alone, and all the people stand by thee from morning unto even?" (Exodus 18:14). In addition to questioning Moses' practice of counseling the people all by himself, Jethro also suggested that Moses' way of doing things was hurting the very people he was trying to help. Moses responded to Jethro's suggestions by explaining his actions: "Because the people come unto me to enquire of God: When they have a matter, they come unto me; and I judge between one and another, and I do make them know the statutes of God, and his laws" (Exodus 18:15–16). Jethro offered counsel that is as applicable today to a busy parent or a burdened Church leader as it was to Moses thousands of years ago:

> The thing that thou doest is not good.
>
> Thou wilt surely wear away, both thou, and this people that is with thee: for this thing is too heavy for thee; thou art not able to perform it thyself alone.
>
> Hearken now unto my voice, I will give thee counsel, and God shall be with thee: Be thou for the people to God-ward, that thou mayest bring the causes unto God:
>
> And thou shalt teach them ordinances and laws, and shalt shew them the way wherein they must walk, and the work that they must do. (Exodus 18:17–20)

Jethro further counseled Moses to invite others to assist him in dealing with the day-to-day concerns of the people, reserving for himself only the most serious problems. He believed that if such a strategy were followed, both Moses and the people would be blessed:

Moreover thou shalt provide out of all the people able men, such as fear God, men of truth, hating covetousness; and place such over them, to be rulers of thousands, and rulers of hundreds, rulers of fifties, and rulers of tens:

And let them judge the people at all seasons: and it shall be, that every great matter they shall bring unto thee, but every small matter they shall judge: so shall it be easier for thyself, and they shall bear the burden with thee.

If thou shalt do this thing, and God command thee so, then thou shalt be able to endure, and all this people shall also go to their place in peace. (Exodus 18:21–23)

Jethro understood that Moses would need to receive the Lord's approval before acting on any of this counsel—which Moses did:

So Moses hearkened to the voice of his father in law, and did all that he had said.

And Moses chose able men out of all Israel, and made them heads over the people, rulers of thousands, rulers of hundreds, rulers of fifties, and rulers of tens.

And they judged the people at all seasons: the hard causes they brought unto Moses, but every small matter they judged themselves.

And Moses let his father in law depart; and he went his way into his own land. (Exodus 18:24–27)

Jethro's counsel contains several important principles that blessed Moses anciently and can bless each of us today as well. Not only was Moses harming himself (and probably his own family) by running faster than he had strength (Mosiah 4:27; D&C 10:4) but he was also creating an unhealthy dependency among the people. Instead of teaching his fellow Israelites to rely upon God and His teachings, upon themselves, and upon their families to solve their problems, they had come to believe that Moses was the only one who could provide them with the help they felt they needed.

President Boyd K. Packer expressed concern about similar dependencies among latter-day Israel:

> We have become very anxious over the amount of counseling that we seem to need in the Church. Our members are becoming dependent.
>
> We must not set up a network of counseling services without at the same time emphasizing the principle of emotional self-reliance and individual independence.
>
> If we lose our emotional and spiritual independence, our self-reliance, we can be weakened quite as much, perhaps even more, than when we become dependent materially.
>
> If we are not careful, we can lose the power of individual revelation.[8]

Much from the interchange between Moses and Jethro can be applied to bringing an appropriate balance to our lives. Some possible applications might include the following:

1. Be open to inspired counsel from others.
2. Delegate, but do not abdicate, in matters that can be appropriately shared with trusted associates.
3. Accept responsibility but do not obsess about matters only you can take care of.
4. Seek the Lord's guidance and approval of the major decisions you make.
5. Learn from the scriptures and teach others to do so as well.
6. Enact your decisions in wisdom and order.

Mary and Martha

The story of Mary and Martha provides us with another important scriptural record of individuals struggling to find balance in their lives. The account of the sisters of Lazarus and their interaction with the Savior has been the subject of some controversy because of questions it appears to raise about the relative importance of our temporal duties and eternal relationships.

The story begins with Jesus visiting the home of Mary, Martha, and Lazarus—two sisters and a brother with whom the Savior had interacted on previous occasions (John 11–12): "Now it came to pass, as they went, that he [Jesus] entered into a certain village: and a certain woman named Martha received him into her house. And she had a sister called Mary, which also sat at Jesus' feet, and heard his word" (Luke 10:38–39).

While Mary was sitting and listening to Jesus speak, Martha was busy with meal preparations, feeling burdened by her sister's choosing not to help her. "But Martha was cumbered [distracted and burdened] about much serving, and came to him, and said, Lord, dost thou not care that my sister hath left me to serve alone? bid her therefore that she help me" (Luke 10:40). Jesus' response to Martha's question indicates that He was concerned about Martha's anxieties with life in general, as well as her negative judgment of her sister, Mary: "And Jesus answered and said unto her, Martha, Martha, thou art careful [anxious] and troubled about many things: But one thing is needful: and Mary hath chosen that good part, which shall not be taken away from her" (Luke 10:41–42).[9]

These verses are rich with meaning and illustrate great keys to understanding how we deal with the day-to-day challenges of life. Like each of us, Martha had "many things" in her life with which she was concerned in addition to the particular challenges described in this text. Jesus gently taught Martha (and each of us as well) that while the anxieties, duties, and challenges of life will come and go, there is "one thing" that is essential and eternal—our relationship with God. Jesus didn't chastise Martha for the work she was doing but reminded her that the food and drink she was preparing would soon be consumed and forgotten. By contrast, those (like Mary) who would partake of the "bread of life" (John 6:35) and the "living water" (John 4:10) would never hunger nor thirst again. Jesus also taught Martha that the relationship Mary was developing with the Lord would "not be taken away from her" (Luke 10:42) but would be eternal.

Sister Patricia Terry Holland described a time when she was reminded of the "one thing" that was "needful" in her life:

Just after my release from the Young Women general presidency in April 1986, I had the opportunity of spending a week in Israel. It had been a very difficult and demanding two years for me. Being a good mother with ample time to succeed at that task has always been my first priority, so I had tried to be a full-time mother to a grade-schooler, a high-schooler, and a son preparing for his mission. I had also tried to be a full-time wife to a staggeringly busy university president. And I had to be as much of a full-time counselor in that general presidency as one living fifty miles from the office could be. But in an important period of forming principles and starting programs, I worried that I wasn't doing enough—and I tried to run a little faster.

Toward the end of my two-year term, my health was going downhill. I was losing weight steadily, and I wasn't sleeping well. My husband and children were trying to bandage me together even as I was trying to do the same for them. We were exhausted. And yet, I kept wondering what I might have done to manage it all better. The Brethren, always compassionate, were watching, and extended a loving release. As grateful as my family and I were for the conclusion of my term of service, I nevertheless felt a loss of association—and, I confess, some loss of identity—with these women whom I had come to love so much. Who was I, and where was I in this welter of demands? Should life be as hard as all this? How successful had I been in my several and competing assignments? Or had I muffed them all? The days after my release were about as difficult as the weeks before it. I didn't have any reserve to call on. My tank was on empty, and I wasn't sure there was a filling station anywhere in sight.

Just a few weeks later my husband had an assignment in Jerusalem, and the Brethren traveling on the assignment requested that I accompany him. "Come on," he said. "You can recuperate in the Savior's land of living water and bread of life." As weary as I was, I packed my bags, believing—or, at the very least, hoping—that the time there would be a healing respite.

On a pristinely clear and beautifully bright day, I sat overlooking the Sea of Galilee and reread the tenth chapter of Luke. But instead of the words on the page, I thought I saw with my mind and heard with my heart these words: "[Pat, Pat, Pat,] thou art careful and troubled about many things." Then the power of pure and personal revelation seized me as I read, "But one thing—only one thing—is truly needful." (See Luke 10:40–41.)

The May sun in Israel is so bright that you feel as if you are sitting on top of the world. I had just visited the spot in Bethoron where the sun stood still for Joshua (see Joshua 10:12), and indeed, on that day it seemed so for me as well. As I sat pondering my problems, I felt that same sun's healing rays like warm liquid pouring into my heart, relaxing, calming, and comforting my troubled soul.

Our loving Father in heaven seemed to be whispering to me, "You don't have to worry over so many things. The one thing that is needful—the *only* thing that is truly needful—is to keep your eyes toward the sun—my Son." Suddenly I had true peace. I knew that my life had always been in his hands, from the very beginning! The sea lying peacefully before my eyes had been tempest-tossed and dangerous—many, many times. All I needed to do was to renew my faith and get a firm grasp of his hand, and *together* we could walk on the water.[10]

Sister Holland's feelings of inadequacy and Martha's feelings of anxiety and resentment were far greater burdens to their lives than were the physical burdens each of them faced. The adversary knows that if he can tempt us to be consumed with lesser issues, as important as many of them may be, he will effectively cut us off from the healing and empowering influence of the Holy Ghost.

The scriptural account of Martha, Mary, and Jesus offers several important keys to balancing our lives. Some of these keys include the following:

1. Our relationship with our Heavenly Father and Jesus Christ should always have highest priority.
2. Our relationships with family and friends are often more important than temporal duties.

3. We must always be on guard against allowing lesser tasks to consume our time and energy and thereby become reasons not to be devoted to those having a higher priority.

4. Gentle reproof is most often superior to harsh correction.

5. Being busy isn't always the best indicator of righteous activity. Sometimes the right thing to do is to be still and listen.

LATTER-DAY IDOLATRY

President Spencer W. Kimball once said, "Whatever thing a man sets his heart and his trust in most is his god; and if his god doesn't also happen to be the true and living God of Israel, that man is laboring in idolatry."[11] The first two of the Ten Commandments remind us of the importance of putting God first in our lives: "Thou shalt have no other gods before me" and "Thou shalt not make unto thee any graven image" (Exodus 20:3–4). Though many interpret these warnings against the worship of false gods and the making of graven images to mean simply that we should not follow the teachings of strange gods, bow before statues, or adorn our homes or ourselves with crucifixes, President Spencer W. Kimball provided more detailed counsel to the Latter-day Saints:

As I study ancient scripture, I am more and more convinced that there is significance in the fact that the commandment "Thou shalt have no other gods before me" is the first of the Ten Commandments.

Few men have ever knowingly and deliberately chosen to reject God and his blessings. Rather, we learn from the scriptures that because the exercise of faith has always appeared to be more difficult than relying on things more immediately at hand, carnal man has tended to transfer his trust in God to material things. Therefore, in all ages when men have fallen under the power of Satan and lost the faith, they have put in its place a hope in the "arm of flesh" and in "gods of silver, and gold, of brass, iron, wood, and stone, which see not, nor hear, nor know" (Dan. 5:23)—that is, in idols. This I find to be a dominant theme in the Old Testament. . . .

The Lord has blessed us as a people with a prosperity unequaled in times past. The resources that have been placed in our power are good, and necessary to our work here on the earth. But I am afraid that many of us have been surfeited with flocks and herds and acres and barns and wealth and have begun to worship them as false gods, and they have power over us. Do we have more of these good things than our faith can stand? Many people spend most of their time working in the service of a self-image that includes sufficient money, stocks, bonds, investment portfolios, property, credit cards, furnishings, automobiles, and the like to *guarantee* carnal security throughout, it is hoped, a long and happy life. Forgotten is the fact that our assignment is to use these many resources in our families and quorums to build up the kingdom of God.[12]

President Kimball gave several examples of idolatry among the Latter-day Saints. His examples included a man who was called to Church service but who declined the invitation because he couldn't take time away from his profession, a young man who declined a mission call because of his love for his vehicle, and of an older couple who put retirement and travel before God:

> An older couple retired from the world of work and also, in effect, from the Church. They purchased a pickup truck and camper and, separating themselves from all obligations, set out to see the world and simply enjoy what little they had accumulated the rest of their days. They had no time for the temple, were too busy for genealogical research and for missionary service. He lost contact with his high priests quorum and was not home enough to work on his personal history. Their experience and leadership were sorely needed in their branch, but, unable to "endure to the end," they were not available.[13]

What is it that we have placed before God? Identifying the false gods we worship will go a long way towards helping us to balance our lives. Sometimes these false gods are easy to identify as evil, but the more difficult idols are the good things that distract us from the right things we ought to be about. Elder Neal A. Maxwell explained:

Striking the proper balance is one of the keenest tests of our agency. Therefore, we need to ask regularly for inspiration in the use of our time and in the making of our daily decisions. So often our hardest choices are between competing and desirable alternatives (each with righteous consequences), when there is *not* time to do both at once. Indeed, it is at the mortal intersections—where time and talent and opportunities meet—that priorities, like traffic lights, are sorely needed. Quiet, sustained goodness is the order of heaven, not conspicuous but episodic busyness.[14]

The apostle Paul used the words of Moses to warn the early Corinthian Saints concerning the worship of an idol we don't often think of as a false god: the worship of pleasure. "Neither be ye idolaters, as were some of them [the ancient children of Israel]; as it is written, The people sat down to eat and drink, and rose up to play" (1 Corinthians 10:7; see also Exodus 32:6). Paul warned Timothy of those who were "lovers of pleasures more than lovers of God" (2 Timothy 3:4). In the Book of Mormon we read Samuel the Lamanite's warning concerning those who "sought for happiness in doing iniquity" (Helaman 13:38).

It is my belief that even wholesome pursuits, if placed above doing God's will, can be idolatrous. Life was not intended to be easy and continually full of fun and frolic. Lehi taught his son Jacob, "For it must needs be, that there is an opposition in all things" (2 Nephi 2:11). The warnings given by President Kimball, the apostle Paul, and Samuel the Lamanite are saying not that travel, fun, recreation, and pleasure should never be a part of our lives but that there is great danger in allowing such pursuits to interfere with our relationship to God, our relationship with our families, and our continuing to build His kingdom.

RUNNING FASTER THAN WE HAVE STRENGTH

The scriptures contain accounts of individuals whose lives lost balance because they were doing too much of a good thing. President Boyd K. Packer warned, "A virtue when pressed to the extreme may turn into a vice."[15] Think of the well-meaning bishop who spends so much of his time counseling ward members that his family, his professional duties, and even himself begin to suffer the consequences. I know from my own experience as a young bishop the serious consequences that came from running faster than I had strength. In addition to the promptings of an all-wise Father in Heaven, the graciousness of Jesus Christ, a devoted wife who reminded me of my responsibilities at home and to myself, and fine counselors, I credit the Book of Mormon and the Joseph Smith Translation of the Bible for helping me understand what it means to keep an ordered balance in serving others. From the teachings of King Benjamin we read:

> I would that ye should impart of your substance to
> the poor, every man according to that which he hath,
> such as feeding the hungry, clothing the naked, visiting

the sick and administering to their relief, both spiritually and temporally, according to their wants.

And see that all these things are done in wisdom and order; for it is not requisite that a man should run faster than he has strength. And again, it is expedient that he should be diligent, that thereby he might win the prize; therefore, all things must be done in order. (Mosiah 4:26–27)

I had mistakenly believed that the answer to most problems was simply to work harder, longer, and later. Hard work and sacrifice will always be an important key to success in our families, professions, and Church assignments, but, as I learned, the Lord would have us serve in His way and not our own.

In the Book of Mormon I read of the importance of respecting the agency of those we are attempting to serve. The prophet Alma wrote of his desire to save all those with whom he labored:

O that I were an angel, and could have the wish of mine heart, that I might go forth and speak with the trump of God, with a voice to shake the earth, and cry repentance unto every people!

Yea, I would declare unto every soul, as with the voice of thunder, repentance and the plan of redemption, that they should repent and come unto our God, that there might not be more sorrow upon all the face of the earth. (Alma 29:1–2)

Then Alma stated, "But behold, I am a man, and do *sin* in my wish" (Alma 29:3; emphasis added). He then explained why what appears to be such a noble wish for him (and, by extension, for me), was a sin: "I ought to be content with the things which the Lord hath allotted unto me. . . . for I know that he granteth unto men according to their desire whether it be unto death or unto life" (Alma 29:3–4).

One of our Latter-day Saint hymns describes this same truth:

> *Know this, that every soul is free*
> *To choose his life and what he'll be;*
> *For this eternal truth is giv'n:*
> *That God will force no man to heav'n.*
>
> *He'll call, persuade, direct aright,*
> *And bless with wisdom, love, and light,*
> *In nameless ways be good and kind,*
> *But never force the human mind.*[16]

I was trying to carry my ward members on my back and by so doing was weakening their ability to rely upon the Lord and thereby gain strength for themselves. Like Moses, I was wearing away because what I was attempting to do was too hard for me to do alone, and I was hurting my ward members by failing to help them prayerfully seek their own answers or solutions.

In addition to the counsel of King Benjamin and Alma, consider the following comparison between the Joseph Smith Translation and the King James Version of this familiar verse:

And whosoever shall compel thee to go a mile, go with him twain. (KJV Matthew 5:41)

And whosoever shall compel thee to go a mile, go with him a mile; and whosoever shall compel thee to go with him twain, thou shalt go with him twain. (JST Matthew 5:43)

There is certainly a time and place to go the second mile, but if we are going two miles when the Lord would have us go only one, we are in danger of "looking beyond the mark" (Jacob 4:14). Experience has taught me that when I look beyond what the Lord would have me do, or in some other way fall short of His expectations, that is when I lose the "fulness of the Holy Ghost" (D&C 109:15) and my life quickly falls out of balance.

I wish I had understood earlier the counsel given by President Harold B. Lee to the bishops of the Church: "Most men do not set priorities to guide them in allocating their time, and most men forget that the first priority should be to maintain their own spiritual and physical strength. Then comes their family, then the Church, and then their professions—and all need time."[17]

If we put God first, He will teach us what should be first, second, third, and so forth. If we seek the Lord's guidance, we might even find that while we will have ordered priorities by which we generally govern our lives, the order of these priorities might change from day to day. The scriptures plainly teach that there is a time and a place to "organize [o]urselves" and "prepare every needful thing" (D&C 88:119). Other times we are to follow Nephi's example when he, upon returning to Jerusalem to obtain the brass plates, describes himself as "[being] led by the Spirit, not knowing beforehand the things which I should do" (1 Nephi 4:6).

COUNTERFEIT SOLUTIONS

It should also be said that the twin principles of "organize yourselves" and "being led by the Spirit" also have their counterfeit applications. The British philosopher C. S. Lewis once observed, "He [the devil] always sends errors into the world in pairs—pairs of opposites."[18] Latter-day Saints may be familiar with cultural stereotypes of LDS women who overprepare and LDS men who underprepare for class and quorum instruction. Sister Jones prepares months in advance for her Relief Society lesson, while Brother Jones takes a few minutes of preparation in the foyer during the hour before it is time to teach his lesson—skipping his Sunday School class to do so. Although there is wisdom in making adequate preparation, Sister Jones's lessons may be so structured that she does not allow the Spirit to guide and perhaps even change what she emphasizes as she teaches her lesson. Also, her hours of preparation may have taken the place of spending needed time with her family or taking care of her own spiritual and physical needs—adding to her feelings of frustration. If Sister Jones isn't wise, her organization may turn to rigidity and may also create an unrealistic standard for others to follow—thus adding to their stress and anxiety.

Brother Jones may defend his style of lesson preparation by the scriptural injunction to "take no thought how or what ye shall speak: for it shall be given you in that same hour what ye shall speak" (Matthew 10:19). Sadly, Brother Jones's lessons may lack the structure necessary to teach the doctrines of the gospel appropriately. If he isn't careful, his spontaneity may turn to chaos and his lessons will not have the spiritual power necessary to inspire and heal. The Lord's perfect blend between organization and being directed by the Spirit is found in the revelation from the Lord to the Prophet Joseph Smith in the early days of the Restoration: "Neither take ye thought beforehand what ye shall say; but treasure up in your minds continually the words of life, and it shall be given you in the very hour that portion that shall be meted unto every man" (D&C 84:85).

Those of us who insist on having every detail ready for a lesson or a talk need to exercise greater faith in the Lord to guide us in what we will say, whereas those of us who are not inclined to prepare diligently need to take the time to continually fill our minds with instruction and allow our hearts to be nurtured through inspiration. Doing so will decrease our own experiences of frustration and contribute to the blessing of others as well, for "it is not the work of God that is frustrated, but the work of men" (D&C 3:3).

CONCLUSION

Many have taken comfort in the promise of the apostle Paul: "There hath no temptation taken you but such as is common to man: but God is faithful, who will not suffer you to be tempted above that ye are able; but will with the temptation also make a way to escape, that ye may be able to bear it" (1 Corinthians 10:13). Yet sooner or later they to come to a point where they find they aren't able to adequately balance the many challenges and burdens that are a part of their lives. Some begin to question the veracity of Paul's promise, the goodness of God, and even His very existence. Some blame themselves, others, or various circumstances for the problems they face and their inability to maintain balance. Some believe that divorce is the answer to their problems, others change employment, some seek to be released from the Church callings, and still others seek counseling and medication or some other means of bringing sanity to their lives.

While some of these options may be a part of the solution, the Savior and His servants have taught that Paul's promise that we will never have more burden than we can bear is conditional upon the strength of our relationship with our Heavenly Father. The prophet Alma taught, "But that ye would humble yourselves before the Lord, and call on his holy name, and *watch and pray continually, that ye may not be tempted above that which ye can bear,* and thus be led by the Holy Spirit, becoming humble, meek, submissive, patient, full of love and all longsuffering" (Alma 13:28; emphasis added).

Even during those times when the difficult decisions we are called upon to make are between choices that both appear to be good, the Lord will help us discern between what is simply good and what is right. Elder John A. Widtsoe reminded us of the lesson we can learn from choices made by Adam and Eve in the Garden of Eden:

> In life all must choose at times. Sometimes, two possibilities are good; neither is evil. Usually, however, one is of greater import than the other. When in doubt, each must choose that which concerns the good of others—the greater law—rather than that which chiefly benefits ourselves—the lesser law. The greater must be balanced against the lesser. The greater must be chosen whether it be law or thing. That was the choice made in Eden.[19]

The Savior has said: "Come unto me, all ye that labour and are heavy laden, and I will give you rest. Take my yoke upon you, and learn of me; for I am meek and lowly in heart: and ye shall find rest unto your souls. For my yoke is easy, and my burden is light" (Matthew 11:28–30). Jesus Christ is the only being to have achieved a perfect balance in mortality. It is to Him we must look, for it is only through Him that we can successfully balance the competing demands of life.

CHAPTER TWO

Is Depression a Sin or a Sickness?

Recent newspaper headlines report and statistics from pharmaceutical companies confirm that Utah residents have the highest use of antidepressants in the nation.[1] Some have taken these statements to mean that because Utah is predominantly Latter-day Saint, membership in The Church of Jesus Christ of Latter-day Saints must be the cause of this unflattering statistic. Nonetheless, another important detail, which doesn't receive nearly as much press, is that research clearly indicates that members of The Church of Jesus Christ are some of the healthiest individuals and families among whom studies have been conducted.[2] In fact, studies show that Latter-day Saints who are true to their faith actually experience less depression than their counterparts of other faiths.[3]

Why, then, do Utahns have such a high rate of use of antidepressants? Perhaps Utah residents are more frequently prescribed antidepressants because they are generally more educated and thus more likely to visit their physician and receive medication. Maybe the reason lies in residents of Utah being less likely to drink alcohol as a means of dealing with problems but see medication as a legitimate way of addressing the sorrows of life. Perhaps Utahns, especially Latter-day Saint Utahns, are more conscious of living "after the manner of happiness" (2 Nephi 5:27) and have a greater motivation to meet the ideal. While the precise reasons for the higher rate of use of antidepressants among Utah residents have yet to be determined, Latter-day Saints can be confident that such reports are not evidence of the evil fruit of their faith.

Having spent a good part of my career defending the faith, I have learned that we must be very careful not to believe that "all is well in Zion" (2 Nephi 28:21), pat ourselves on the back, and close our eyes and hearts to individuals and families who, while being in the statistical minority, are also in the spiritual majority—human beings in pain and in need of love, not judgment. Prophetic commentary and scriptural teachings help us to understand such issues as the relationship of sin to depression, along with the related influences of body chemistry and family dynamics. Related issues include the role of medication and other forms of therapy in the treatment of depression as well as how a person who is suffering with depression can better apply the teachings of the gospel—particularly the atonement of Jesus Christ—to his or her individual circumstances.

THE "BLACK PLAGUE" OF DEPRESSION

Most would agree that our pioneer ancestors faced the kinds of challenges that make those of us living in this generation grateful we were born when we were. Persecution, pestilence, death, disease, drought, crippling accidents, hunger, freezing cold, and sweltering heat were only a part of the heavy burden they were called to bear. It is humbling to consider that much of the ease we enjoy today came because of the sacrifice of those who have gone before. It has been said, "One generation plants the trees, and another gets the shade." In so many ways we are living in the shade of sacrifice provided by those who lived before us. I often think of the great legacy created by those who left lives of relative ease to respond to the Savior's call to build the kingdom of God. I marvel at courageous women and children who supported faithful husbands and fathers while they were serving missions far from home. On a personal note, it is humbling to realize that it was common for bishops and stake presidents to serve in their callings for thirty or forty years. Those were difficult times, matched by equally courageous and faithful individuals and families.

Though we may not face the same kinds of challenges our pioneer ancestors faced, Elder M. Russell Ballard has pointed out that the Saints in our day face monumental challenges of a different kind:

> Although our journeys today are less demanding physically than the trek of our pioneers 150 years ago, they are no less challenging. Certainly it was hard to walk across a continent to establish a new home in a dry western desert. But who can say if that was any more difficult than is the task of living faithful, righteous lives in today's

confusingly sinful world, where the trail is constantly shifting and where divine markers of right and wrong are being replaced by political expediency and diminishing morality. The road we travel today is treacherous, and the scriptures tell us it will continue to be so until the very end.[4]

Commenting specifically on the emotional challenges faced by those living in our day, Elder Jeffrey R. Holland states:

> Life in every era has had its troubles. Surely the Dark Ages were appropriately named, and not one of us is anxious to be transported back even to those later years of, say, the Hundred Years War or the Black Plague. No, we're quite happy to have been born in a century of unprecedented material blessings and abundant living; yet in community after community, in small nations and large, we see individuals and families facing heightened anxiety and fear. It would seem that discouragement, depression, and despair are our contemporary "Black Plague." Ours is, as Jesus said it would be, a time of distress with perplexity (see Luke 21:25).[5]

It is estimated that each year in the United States of America alone, 17 million people experience the "plague" of depression. Elder Alexander B. Morrison, an emeritus member of the First Quorum of the Seventy, estimates in his book *Valley of Sorrow: A Layman's Guide to Understanding Mental Illness* that "more than one in ten people will suffer a serious depression at some time during their lives."[6] As anyone who has had a close relationship with someone who suffers with depression will tell you, depression affects not only the person experiencing it but has a tremendous effect on family, friends, and others as well. Depression is a serious problem in need of our most serious attention.

DEPRESSION DEFINED

Major depression needs to be differentiated from "godly sorrow" (2 Corinthians 7:10) or simply having "the blues"—feelings experienced by most everyone one time or another. In my experience as a therapist and as an ecclesiastical leader, it is not unusual for individuals to apologize for their tears as we speak of something that is painful to them. In my attempts to comfort them, I often respond, "No need to apologize. 'Jesus wept' (John 11:35), and so may you." Sometimes we will discuss the doctrinal truth that sadness and the shedding of tears are two of the attributes of God that remind us that we are His children. In the Pearl of Great Price we find an extraordinary exchange between the prophet Enoch and the Lord concerning His sorrowing and tears over the wickedness of the inhabitants of the earth. Enoch was surprised at the Lord's expression of sorrow.

> And it came to pass that the God of heaven looked upon the residue of the people, and he wept; and Enoch bore record of it, saying: *How is it that the heavens weep, and shed forth their tears as the rain upon the mountains?*

And Enoch said unto the Lord: *How is it that thou canst weep,* seeing thou art holy, and from all eternity to all eternity?

And were it possible that man could number the particles of the earth, yea, millions of earths like this, it would not be a beginning to the number of thy creations; and thy curtains are stretched out still; and yet thou art there, and thy bosom is there; and also thou art just; thou art merciful and kind forever;

And thou hast taken Zion to thine own bosom, from all thy creations, from all eternity to all eternity; and naught but peace, justice, and truth is the habitation of thy throne; and mercy shall go before thy face and have no end; *how is it thou canst weep?* (Moses 7:28–31; emphasis added)

In essence, Enoch was saying, "You are the God of the universe. How can *You* cry?" The Lord's response is a tender representation of His love for His children.

The Lord said unto Enoch: Behold these thy brethren; they are the workmanship of mine own hands, and I gave unto them their knowledge, in the day I created them; and in the Garden of Eden, gave I unto man his agency;

And unto thy brethren have I said, and also given commandment, that they should love one another, and that they should choose me, their Father; but behold, they are without affection, and they hate their own blood. (Moses 7:32–33)

Most parents experience grief at the loss of a child—whether that loss is physically, emotionally, or spiritually. Life is painful, and all of us experience sadness related to a host of different kinds of losses. To do so is an expression of our divine origin and is part of what it means to be a son or daughter of heavenly parents. Elder Boyd K. Packer has taught that sadness, disappointment, and failure are a necessary part of the human experience:

> We live in a day when the adversary stresses on every hand the philosophy of instant gratification. We seem to demand *instant* everything, including instant solutions to our problems. We are indoctrinated that somehow we should always be instantly emotionally comfortable. When that is not so, some become anxious—and all too frequently seek relief from counseling, from analysis, and even from medication. It was meant to be that life would be a challenge. To suffer some anxiety, some depression, some disappointment, even some failure is normal. Teach our members that if they have a good, miserable day once in a while, or several in a row, to stand steady and face them. Things will straighten out. There is great purpose in our struggle in life.[7]

MAJOR DEPRESSIVE DISORDER

Although there is a form of sadness that is of God and is actually a necessary part of the life experience that will help us to become more like Him, there is another experience called "major depressive disorder" or "clinical depression" that if not addressed has the potential to drive us away from God and from any meaningful relationship with others. This depression is often characterized by the following symptoms experienced over a prolonged period of time:

1. Poor appetite or significant weight loss or weight gain (not associated with a diet).
2. Inability to sleep or a desire always to sleep.
3. Restlessness and/or loss of energy.
4. Loss of interest or pleasure in activities once enjoyed.
5. Feelings of worthlessness or inappropriate guilt.
6. Diminished ability to think clearly.
7. Recurring thoughts of death.[8]

Individuals who continually suffer such problems are in need of help and might want to consider talking to their bishop, receiving his counsel, and possibly seeking a referral for an evaluation and possible treatment through LDS Family Services or from some other well-trained professional. The Prophet Joseph Smith stated, "A man can do nothing for himself unless God direct him in the right way; and the Priesthood is for that purpose."[9]

Priesthood involvement is important; even if individuals in

need receive professional treatment, they would be blessed by working with their bishop as well, at least periodically. Remember the words of Alma, "Trust no one to be your teacher nor your minister, except he be a man of God, walking in his ways and keeping his commandments" (Mosiah 23:14). As with other professionals, not all therapists are of equal ability—some can provide great help, and others can do more harm than good. It is critical that the person in need receive help from someone who is both *faithful* and *competent,* as there are those who are faithful but not well trained and those who are very competent but not faithful. LDS Family Services has been given the commission to help make such judgments and can be accessed through a bishop's referral.

SCRIPTURAL EXAMPLES OF INDIVIDUALS SUFFERING WITH DEPRESSION

The scriptures contain numerous examples of individuals who experienced and overcame what could be described as major depression. In the Old Testament we find the story of Hannah, the mother of the prophet Samuel. Before Hannah gave birth to Samuel, she suffered many difficult years because of her inability to have children. Hannah was also burdened by the constant criticism of her husband's other wife, Peninnah. The scriptural account begins by describing the difficult events surrounding the yearly trip made by Elkanah and his wives to the temple to worship and offer sacrifice:

> And this man went up out of his city yearly to wor-
> ship and to sacrifice unto the Lord of hosts in Shiloh. . . .
>
> And when the time was that Elkanah offered [sacri-
> fice at the temple], he gave to Peninnah his wife, and to
> all her sons and her daughters, portions [of the sacrifice]:
>
> But unto Hannah he gave a worthy portion; for he
> loved Hannah: but the Lord had shut up her womb.
>
> And her adversary [Peninnah] also provoked her sore,
> for to make her fret, because the Lord had shut up her
> womb.
>
> And as he did so year by year, when she went up to
> the house of the Lord, so she provoked her; therefore she
> wept, and did not eat. (1 Samuel 1:3–7)

Elkanah attempted to comfort her by saying, "Hannah,
why weepest thou? and why eatest thou not? and why is thy
heart grieved? *am* not I better to thee than ten sons?" (1
Samuel 1:8).

Though Hannah's response is not recorded, it is evident
that her husband's attempt to comfort her by encouraging her
to count her blessings was unsuccessful. She continued to seek
relief through prayer:

> And she was in bitterness of soul, and prayed unto
> the Lord, and wept sore.
>
> And she vowed a vow, and said, O Lord of hosts, if
> thou wilt indeed look on the affliction of thine hand-
> maid, and remember me, and not forget thine handmaid,
> but wilt give unto thine handmaid a man child, then I

will give him unto the Lord all the days of his life, and there shall no razor come upon his head. (1 Samuel 1:10–11)

Eli, the presiding priest at the temple, observed Hannah's grief-filled prayer and concluded that she was drunk:

> And it came to pass, as she continued praying before the Lord, that Eli marked [observed] her mouth.
> Now Hannah, she spake in her heart; only her lips moved, but her voice was not heard: therefore Eli thought she had been drunken. (1 Samuel 1:12–13)

The use of alcohol as a means of dealing with despair appears to have been a problem then as it is now, but Hannah knew better. Her despair, while difficult to bear, had become her motivation to turn to the only legitimate source of healing she knew—God. The next several verses describe the instructive conversation between Hannah and Eli:

> And Eli said unto her, How long wilt thou be drunken? put away thy wine from thee.
> And Hannah answered and said, No, my lord, I *am* a woman of a sorrowful spirit: I have drunk neither wine nor strong drink, but have poured out my soul before the Lord.
> Count not thine handmaid for a daughter of Belial [wickedness or worthlessness]: for out of the abundance of my complaint and grief have I spoken hitherto. (1 Samuel 1:14–16)

Eli then instructed and promised Hannah: "Go in peace: and the God of Israel grant thee thy petition that thou hast asked of him." Hannah responded in faith, "Let thine hand-maid find grace in thy sight." We then learn that Hannah "went her way, and did eat, and her countenance was no more sad" (1 Samuel 1:17–18).

Hannah and Elkanah returned home, Hannah conceived, and in due time she gave birth to Samuel. Hannah was true to the vow she had made before Samuel was conceived, for at the appropriate time she took him to the temple and "lent him to the Lord" (1 Samuel 1:28). This action demonstrates that the vow she took during her depressed state represented her love for the Lord and was not simply a way of bargaining with God to fulfill her own desires. It is also remarkable, perhaps even miraculous, to note that Hannah's despair lifted before, not after, she was blessed with the child she wanted so desperately. It appears that Hannah's despair was swept away, at least in part, because of her confidence in the promise given to her by the Lord through one of His authorized servants.

THE DOCTRINE OF THE SOUL

Was Hannah's despair a result of sin or was it godly sorrow over her inability to fulfill her worthy desire to be a mother? Is faith in God and obedience to His commandments sufficient to free us from the emotional problems so many of us face? If Hannah were living in our day, would it be appropriate for her to receive professional counseling and possibly medication?

One of the "plain and precious" (1 Nephi 13:28) doctrines

taken from the earth by apostasy and restored to the earth through latter-day scripture is the teaching that "the spirit and the body are the soul of man" (D&C 88:15). Elder James E. Talmage taught:

> It is peculiar to the theology of the Latter-day Saints that we regard the body as an essential part of the soul. Read your dictionaries, the lexicons, and encyclopedias, and you will find that nowhere, outside of the Church of Jesus Christ, is the solemn and eternal truth taught that the soul of man is the body and the spirit combined.[10]

This statement has great relevance to both the diagnosis and the treatment of depression. There are some exceptions, of course, but the experience of depression is best understood as having both physical and spiritual dimensions. To neglect either dimension of our soul is to fail to address our true identity. One of the greatest tragedies I have witnessed is to see someone whose "despair cometh because of iniquity" (Moroni 10:22) being treated solely through professional counseling and medication. Such individuals are in desperate need of the peace that can come only through the repentance and forgiveness made possible through the healing power of Christ. Most bishops and many therapists could tell you of individuals who in spite of years of counseling and medication were able to find peace only after coming to Christ through sincere repentance and forgiveness.

On the other hand, there are also those whose depression is physical in nature but have been led to believe that all forms of therapy outside reading the scriptures, praying, and so forth are of the devil. Most therapists and many Church leaders could give examples of such individuals who have benefited greatly from inspired, clinical intervention. Elder Alexander B. Morrison has counseled:

> We should not underestimate the effectiveness of medication, which has helped untold millions of those with mental illness to come back to reality, overcome despair, regain hope, quell their inner demons, and live useful and productive lives. . . . It seems obvious that both medication and psychotherapy have invaluable roles to play.[11]

I am cautious about completely equating depression with physical problems, such as diabetes, although it has become the socially acceptable thing to do. Though some people do suffer from depression that is totally physical in origin (like diabetes), and others have feelings of despair rooted solely in things spiritual, most depression is a combination of both (which is not true with many physical diseases). An acquaintance of mine, a psychiatrist, speaks disparagingly of Church leaders because of their emphasis on sin and repentance. Another acquaintance, a man who considers himself very faithful, continually speaks evil of psychiatrists, psychologists, and social workers because of their emphasis on counseling and medication. If we measure the equally biased perspectives of my two friends against the standard of doctrine, we find they are both misguided, because "the spirit and the body are the soul of man" (D&C

88:15). Both the spiritual and the physical dimensions of our lives need to be given serious consideration when dealing with depression, and for that matter, most any other problem as well. Purely physical ailments can be better dealt with if one is spiritually strong, and the resolution of spiritual problems can be greatly enhanced if one is physically strong.

In speaking of both physical and spiritual origins of depression, President Boyd K. Packer stated: "We know that some anxiety and depression is caused by physical disorders, but much (perhaps most) of it is not pain of the body but of the spirit. Spiritual pain resulting from guilt can be replaced with peace of mind."[12] President Packer, while acknowledging the physical dimension of some anxiety and depression, emphasizes the spiritual dimension because it is guilt that brings the greatest despair and the Holy Ghost that will bring us the greatest happiness.

Speaking of the power of the Holy Ghost, President James E. Faust has said:

> I believe the Spirit of the Holy Ghost is the greatest guarantor of inward peace in our unstable world. It can be more mind-expanding and can make us have a better sense of well-being than any chemical or other earthly substance. It will calm nerves; it will breathe peace to our souls. This Comforter can be with us as we seek to improve. It can function as a source of revelation to warn us of impending danger and also help keep us from making mistakes. It can enhance our natural senses so that we

can see more clearly, hear more keenly, and remember what we should remember. It is a way of maximizing our happiness.[13]

THE PROPER PLACE OF REPENTANCE

God has given His teachings as a means by which we can become like Him. Every commandment God has given is an expression of who He is. When we live in harmony with who God is by following what He has taught, His Spirit touches us as a witness that we are on the right path. When we act contrary to God's will (sin), the Spirit withdraws and we feel the absence of God. Though many of us regard sin as the breaking of one of the major commandments (and it is), it can also be as simple as harboring a grudge, exaggerating one's success, nursing a hurt or self-pity, or coveting another's beauty, title, or position. The scriptures also imply that sin can be something we are doing (or failing to do) out of ignorance (3 Nephi 6:18). Consider the story of Esther:

> Esther was trying to be the perfect wife and mother. Every morning she woke up announcing to herself: "This is the day I will be perfect. The house will be organized, I will not yell at my children, and I will finish everything important I have planned." Every night she went to bed discouraged, because she had failed to accomplish her goal. She became irritable with everyone, including herself, and she began to wonder what she was doing wrong.
>
> One night Esther knelt in prayer and asked for

guidance. Afterward, while lying awake, a startling thought came to her. She realized that in focusing on her own perfection she was focusing on herself and failing to love others, particularly her husband and children. She was being not loving, therefore not Christlike, but essentially selfish. She was trying to be sweet to her children, not freely, out of love for them, but because she saw it as a necessary part of *her* perfection. Furthermore, she was trying to get a feeling of righteousness by forcing her husband and children to meet her ideal of perfection. When her children got in the way of her "perfect" routine, she blamed them for making her feel "imperfect," and she became irritated with them and treated them in a most unloving way. Likewise, if her husband did not meet her idea of perfection when he came home from work, she judged him as failing and was critical of him as a way of reinforcing her sense of her own righteousness.

Esther remembered the Savior's commandment to be perfect *as he is perfect* (see 3 Nephi 12:48). She realized that this perfection includes loving as he loved (John 13:34), and realized she had been pursuing the wrong goal.[14]

Esther's frustration could in time have turned to despair because she was basing her happiness on her husband's and children's compliance with her wishes. Esther was not guilty of sin in the traditional sense of the term, but she was suffering the consequences of failing to live in harmony with the Savior and His teachings. While we can hope Esther's husband and children made some changes of their own, Esther's realization of the shallowness of her behavior and subsequent change could also be described as *revelation* and *repentance*. Though the word *repentance* may seem to have some ominous overtones, it simply means "change." In the LDS Bible Dictionary we read: "The Greek word [metanoia] of which this is the translation denotes a change of mind, i.e., a fresh view about God, about oneself, and about the world. Since we are born into conditions of mortality, repentance comes to mean a turning of the heart and will to God, and a renunciation of sin to which we are naturally inclined."[15]

In her own mind, Esther certainly wasn't being sinful; she was simply trying to help her husband and children be better people. Through the Holy Ghost, however, she came to understand that she wasn't treating them as the Savior would have her treat them, and she had a change of heart. If Esther hadn't come to understand the importance of following Christ and her own divine potential, she could have gone on to become angry and even depressed over her less-than-ideal husband and children.

Another individual described the process of repentance as follows:

> I used to view repentance as punishment, as something I had to do because I had been bad. In actuality, repentance is a process of growth and change. As our will is turned toward God, we become aligned with Him and His commandments. Then the powers of heaven can flow

freely. Repentance brings freedom from the natural self, allowing the body to conform to the true self.[16]

Elder Maxwell has taught, "If we understood the nature of repentance better, there would be more of it!"[17] The changes involved in the repentance process are often small. In the Doctrine and Covenants we read, "Out of small things proceedeth that which is great" (64:33). Changes in diet (D&C 89), exercise (1 Timothy 4:8), friendships (2 Thessalonians 3:14–15), and sleep schedules (D&C 88:124) may not be seen as repentance by some, but in practice they can be some of the changes necessary to address the problems we are facing.

Our prophets have clearly taught that we are the sons and daughters of God with the potential to become like Him. Elder Dallin H. Oaks has spoken of the antidepressant value of coming to know our divine identity:

> Consider the power of the idea taught in our beloved song "I Am a Child of God" (*Hymns,* 1985, no. 301). . . . Here is the answer to one of life's great questions, "Who am I?" I am a child of God with a spirit lineage to heavenly parents. That parentage defines our eternal potential. That powerful idea is a potent antidepressant. It can strengthen each of us to make righteous choices and to seek the best that is within us. Establish in the mind of a young person the powerful idea that he or she is a child of God and you have given self-respect and motivation to move against the problems of life.[18]

Yes, depression can result from breaking the commandments of God (Moroni 10:22), but we must always take seriously both the spirit and the body in the causes and cures of depression. President Boyd K. Packer has described what it is like to live in ignorance of a blessing that is readily available but that we, through our ignorance, miss obtaining:

> So many live with accusing guilt when relief is ever at hand. So many are like the immigrant woman who skimped and saved and deprived herself until, by selling all of her possessions, she bought a steerage-class ticket to America. She rationed out the meager provisions she was able to bring with her. Even so, they were gone early in the voyage. When others went for their meals, she stayed below deck—determined to suffer through it. Finally, on the last day, she must, she thought, afford one meal to give her strength for the journey yet ahead. When she asked what the meal would cost, she was told that all of the meals had been included in the price of her ticket.[19]

President Packer's words poignantly illustrate how we through our ignorance can miss the life-giving and life-sustaining power of the atonement of Christ. His story also illustrates how we can suffer unnecessarily because of our ignorance of the blessings provided by medical science.

President Brigham Young counseled us on the relationship between both spiritual and physical treatments:

You may go to some people here, and ask what ails them, and they answer, "I don't know, but we feel a dreadful distress in the stomach and in the back; we feel all out of order, and we wish you to lay hands upon us." "Have you used any remedies?" "No. We wish the Elders to lay hands upon us, and we have faith that we shall be healed." That is very inconsistent according to my faith. If we are sick, and ask the Lord to heal us, and to do all for us that is necessary to be done, according to my understanding of the Gospel of salvation, I might as well ask the Lord to cause my wheat and corn to grow, without my plowing the ground and casting in the seed. It appears consistent to me to apply every remedy that comes within the range of my knowledge, and to ask my Father in heaven, in the name of Jesus Christ, to sanctify that application to the healing of my body; to another this may appear inconsistent.[20]

This is not to say that we should mindlessly trust all that is offered to us in the name of either science or religion. In Galatians 5:20 the English word *witchcraft* is used to translate the Greek word *pharmakei*—from which the English word *pharmacy* is derived. The choice to take or not to take medication is one that should not be made lightly. Medication can be a blessing, or it can be a way of simply treating the symptoms and failing to identify and address the root causes of the problem.

Scriptures and the words of latter-day prophets contain many warnings against heeding those whose teachings have a "form of godliness" (Joseph Smith–History 1:19) but whose doctrine is not pure. The Savior warned of these people on both sides of the debate when He said, "Beware of false prophets, which come to you in sheep's clothing, but inwardly they are ravening wolves" (Matthew 7:15).

THE HEALING POWER OF THE DOCTRINES OF CHRIST

The Book of Mormon plainly teaches that the healing power made possible through the atonement of Christ has application to our physical as well as to our spiritual afflictions. The prophet Alma described these dimensions of the infinite atonement:

> And he shall go forth, suffering pains and afflictions and temptations of every kind; and this that the word might be fulfilled which saith he will take upon him the pains and the sicknesses of his people.
>
> And he will take upon him death, that he may loose the bands of death which bind his people; and he will take upon him their infirmities, that his bowels may be filled with mercy, according to the flesh, that he may know according to the flesh how to succor his people according to their infirmities. (Alma 7:11–12)

Another word for *atonement* is *reconciliation* (Romans 5:10; Hebrews 5:12). Both words imply a "coming together" or an "at-one-ment." Not only does the atonement of Jesus Christ allow us to be reconciled to God but it also makes reconciliation possible between husbands and wives, brothers and sisters, parents and children, neighbors, and even nations. Could it be that if we are not "appointed unto death" (D&C 42:48), the Atonement is also the power that allows our bodies to heal—the reconciliation of cells, tissues, and organs—as well as to reconcile with God?

The Savior taught His disciples that physical illness is not always caused by sinful behavior:

> And as Jesus passed by, he saw a man which was blind from his birth. And his disciples asked him, saying, Master, who did sin, this man, or his parents, that he was born blind? Jesus answered, Neither hath this man sinned, nor his parents: but that the works of God should be made manifest in him. (John 9:1–3; see also 5:17–26)

Elder Boyd K. Packer has taught that it is not always possible to identify the origin of the various problems we face:

> There is another part of us, not so tangible, but quite as real as our physical body. This intangible part of us is described as mind, emotion, intellect, temperament, and many other things. Very seldom is it described as spiritual. But there is a *spirit* in man; to ignore it is to ignore reality. There are spiritual disorders, too, and spiritual diseases that can cause intense suffering. The body and the spirit of man are bound together. Often, very often, when there are disorders, it is very difficult to tell which is which.[21]

Because it is often difficult to tell whether feelings of depression are a manifestation of a physical disorder, a spiritual problem, or a combination of both, we need to do the best we can to give adequate attention to every aspect of our lives. We also need to remember the Lord's counsel to "set in order your own house" (D&C 93:43). Feelings of depression are often the manifestations of family or other relationships that need attention.

President Ezra Taft Benson provided important counsel for dealing with despair in a general conference address entitled "Do Not Despair": "To help us from being overcome by the devil's designs of despair, discouragement, depression, and despondency, the Lord has provided at least a dozen ways which, if followed, will lift our spirits and send us on our way rejoicing."[22] The twelve suggestions are as follows:

1. Repentance (Moroni 10:22)
2. Prayer (D&C 10:5)
3. Service (Luke 9:24)
4. Work (Genesis 3:19)
5. Physical health (D&C 88:124)
6. Reading (Jacob 2:8)
7. Blessings (James 5:14–15)
8. Fasting (Matthew 17:14–21)
9. Friends (D&C 121:9–11)
10. Music (1 Samuel 16:14–23)
11. Endurance (2 Nephi 1:20)
12. Goals (3 Nephi 27:27)

Some have criticized President Benson's counsel as "too simplistic" to deal with the complex problem of depression for which, they believe, the answers will come through more sophisticated means. The prophet Nephi taught that many of the ancient Israelites were lost because of their unwillingness to live the simple truths of the gospel:

> And he did straiten them in the wilderness with his rod; for they hardened their hearts, even as ye have; and the Lord straitened them because of their iniquity. He sent fiery flying serpents among them; and after they were bitten he prepared a way that they might be healed; and the labor which they had to perform was to look; and because of the simpleness of the way, or the easiness of it, there were many who perished (1 Nephi 17:41).

Elder Neal A. Maxwell has observed:

> We like intellectual embroidery. We like complexity because it gives us an excuse for failure, that is, as you increase the complexity of a belief system, you provide more and more refuges for those who don't want to comply; you thereby increase the number of excuses that people can make for failure to comply, and you create a sophisticated intellectual structure which causes people to talk about the gospel instead of doing it. But the gospel of Jesus Christ is not complex. It strips us of any basic excuse for noncompliance, and yet many of us are forever trying to make it more complex.[23]

It is true that some experiences with depression may require the most sophisticated and complex treatments the helping professions can offer, but we should also continue to live the principles of the gospel as taught by the Lord through His servants. The Savior taught this principle when He counseled, "These ought ye to have done, and not to leave the other undone" (Matthew 23:23). We can continue to live the gospel while receiving help from other inspired sources as well. President Joseph F. Smith once said: "Every natural law or scientific principle that man has truly discovered, but which was always known to God, is a part of the gospel truth. There never was and never will be any conflict between truth revealed by the Lord to his servants, the prophets, and truth revealed by him to the scientist, who makes his discoveries through his research and study."[24]

HEALTHY AND UNHEALTHY GUILT

The principal concern in talking about depression in terms of sin and repentance is the tendency to invite sufferers to experience unnecessary feelings of guilt and shame—especially when their specific problem is more physical than spiritual. The danger in talking about depression in terms of chemical imbalances and dysfunctional families is that sufferers may not feel the need to look within and change what needs changing—especially when their problem is more spiritual than physical. Elder Boyd K. Packer acknowledged how feelings of guilt can be a blessing or a burden:

> You have an alarm system built into both body and spirit. In your body it is pain; in your spirit it is guilt—or

spiritual pain. While neither pain nor guilt is pleasant, and an excess of either can be destructive, both are a protection, for they sound the alarm "Don't do that again!"

Be grateful for both. If the nerve endings in your hands were altered so that you couldn't feel pain, you might put them in fire or machinery and destroy them. In your . . . heart of hearts, you know right from wrong (see 2 Nephi 2:5). Learn to pay attention to that spiritual voice of warning within you. Even then you will not get by without some mistakes.[25]

Some would have us dismiss the experience of guilt altogether, believing it to be an artifact of unhealthy religion. But if we understand that some guilt is from God, a guilt that we can appropriately respond to and not legitimately dismiss, it can be a great blessing to us.

The apostle Paul taught the Corinthian Saints, "For godly sorrow worketh repentance to salvation not to be repented of: but the sorrow of the world worketh death" (2 Corinthians 7:10). Earlier in the same epistle, Paul described one of the local Church members being burdened with "overmuch sorrow" and asked the Saints to "confirm your love toward him" (2 Corinthians 2:7–8; see also D&C 121:43). Feelings of remorse for what we have done (guilt) can lead to feelings of despair over who we are (shame). Though guilt is a significant factor in depression, shame is an even more ominous part of what has been described as major depression. Some try to address their guilt and shame by becoming involved in unhealthy relationships that offer acceptance in the beginning but eventually enslave them in the end. Others numb themselves through such things as alcohol and other drugs, food, shopping, pornography, or sexual perversions. Others may try to distract themselves from guilt and shame by making extraordinary personal sacrifices, service, or achievement of one kind or another, attempting to make up for what they have done and for who they feel they should be. Eventually, these strategies fail, and those suffering are left in despair.

CENTERED IN CHRIST

Even though we may employ many effective strategies to deal with depression—some medical and some theological—any strategy, theory, therapy, philosophy, or teaching, if not consistent with the teachings of Jesus Christ, will eventually fail. The Savior taught the Nephites, "But if it be not built upon my gospel, and is built upon the works of men, or upon the works of the devil, verily I say unto you they have joy in their works for a season, and by and by the end cometh, and they are hewn down and cast into the fire, from whence there is no return" (3 Nephi 27:11).

Whether the feelings of depression we experience are biological in origin, spiritual, familial, or a combination of several factors, at some point in our lives each of us must make the decision to give ourselves to God. C. S. Lewis wisely observed:

> Our real selves are all waiting for us in Him. The more I resist Him and try to live on my own, the more I

become dominated by my own heredity and upbringing and surroundings and natural desires. . . . It is when I turn to Christ, when I give myself up to His Personality, that I first begin to have a real personality of my own.[26]

In the sermon at the temple, the Savior taught the ancient Nephites, "Yea, blessed are the poor in spirit *who come unto me, for theirs is the kingdom of heaven*" (3 Nephi 12:3; emphasis added). Notice how those words found in the Book of Mormon differ from the words in the New Testament: "Blessed are the poor in spirit: for theirs is the kingdom of heaven" (Matthew 5:3). The answer to being poor in spirit is to come unto Him. Elsewhere, the Savior counseled, "Come unto me, all ye that labour and are heavy laden, and I will give you rest. Take my yoke upon you, and learn of me; for I am meek and lowly in heart: and ye shall find rest unto your souls. For my yoke is easy, and my burden is light" (Matthew 11:28–30).

When Church members are interviewed by their priesthood leaders to receive a recommend to enter the temple, they are asked if they feel that they are worthy to enter the temple and to take part in the ordinances therein. It has been my experience that many people will modestly respond to such a question by saying something like, "I have a lot of weaknesses, and I am far from perfect, but I guess I feel okay about answering 'yes' to the question." I am always touched by the sincerity and humility of their reply, but I generally probe just a little to make sure they understand the doctrine of the atonement of Christ. If they understand that doctrine, have accepted Christ, and are sincerely trying to follow Him, they have no need to be shy about declaring their worthiness, because worthiness is so much more about "the righteousness of the Redeemer" (2 Nephi 2:3) than it is about us. A number of scriptural texts teach this gracious and merciful truth, but one that I love is found in the Lord's counsel to the Church through the Prophet Joseph Smith. Note that it is the atonement of Christ that will be emphasized at Judgment Day, not our own good works:

> Listen to him who is the advocate with the Father, who is pleading your cause before him—
> Saying: Father, behold the sufferings and death of him who did no sin, in whom thou wast well pleased; behold the blood of thy Son which was shed, the blood of him whom thou gavest that thyself might be glorified;
> Wherefore, Father, spare these my brethren that believe on my name, that they may come unto me and have everlasting life. (D&C 45:3–5)

Years ago, during the oral defense of my doctoral dissertation, I was confronted with a host of questions I had a difficult time answering. I could feel my chances for passing this critical examination slipping away. Just when I felt that I had failed and despair was beginning to overwhelm me, a member of the committee who had assisted me through the dissertation process asked if he could speak. My dear mentor and colleague, Professor Richard N. Williams, took the next twenty minutes and defended all that I had done. The mood of the room quickly changed, a vote was taken, and I passed. As Richard spoke, I felt, probably for the first in my life, what it meant to have an advocate. From that day on, Richard has been a symbol of God's love for me. Even now, whenever I see Brother Williams or talk to him on the phone, I remember his Christlike compassion and exceptional brilliance in defending my work. I wasn't worthy of his *gracious* help, but *mercifully,* Richard ensured that I received the reward I sought—truly a noble "typifying" of the love of Christ (2 Nephi 11:4).

This story, though containing many similarities, differs in one very important way from how Judgment Day will be for you and for me. The Savior as our advocate with the Father will indeed plead our cause, but instead of putting forth our personal righteousness as evidence of our worthiness to enter the celestial kingdom, He will declare that the righteousness that allows us to enter therein is His righteousness—not ours. We can claim His righteousness as our own by taking upon ourselves His name, always remembering Him, and keeping His commandments (D&C 20:77–79), for we must realize that "it is by grace that we are saved, after all we can do" (2 Nephi 25:23).

CONCLUSION

Medical science has made great strides in the past, and we can be confident that the wonderful men and women of science will continue to make progress in years to come regarding the treatment of the latter-day plague of depression. Because we are both spirit and body, because some forms of depression "[come] because of iniquity" (Moroni 10:22), and because our mortal bodies are greatly influenced by the fall of

Adam and Eve, it is vital that we always remember the healing power of the atonement of Jesus Christ in addressing the problems we face. Jesus Christ has power to heal "all manner of sickness and all manner of disease among the people" (Matthew 4:23). Whether our experience with depression is a sickness that has no relationship to sin, or a consequence of the iniquity spoken of in scripture, or some varied combination of both, one thing we can know for certain is that the Savior of the world desires that we be healed:

> And it came to pass that when he had thus spoken, all the multitude, with one accord, did go forth with their sick and their afflicted, and their lame, and with their blind, and with their dumb, and with all them that were afflicted in any manner; and he did heal them every one as they were brought forth unto him.
>
> And they did all, both they who had been healed and they who were whole, bow down at his feet, and did worship him; and as many as could come for the multitude did kiss his feet, insomuch that they did bathe his feet with their tears. (3 Nephi 17:9–10)

CHAPTER THREE

"Can Ye Be Angry, and Not Sin?"

Anger is one of humankind's most common and most
destructive emotional disturbances, and it is one of the central characteristics of most diagnosed emotional disorders.[1]
Anger is generally at the center of many of the problems faced
in marriages, families, and communities throughout the world.
In the United States, for instance, from 1960 through the
1990s, violent crime has increased 560 percent and divorce
rates have quadrupled.[2] Those statistics mirror what has happened in most communities and countries throughout the
world. The expression of anger and the experience of contention, which were once condemned by society, are now
becoming accepted and even encouraged by many as appropriate styles of expression and interaction.

The scriptures plainly teach that come Judgment Day
we will be "judged every man according to their works"
(Revelation 20:13). In the Book of Mormon we learn that we
will be judged according to our thoughts and words, as well as

our deeds (Mosiah 4:30). The Book of Mormon also contains profound insight concerning the controversial question about whether the emotion of anger is a sin. Scripture and the teachings of latter-day prophets give us good counsel concerning anger, a part of the human experience with which we are all familiar.

It has been said that Benjamin Franklin once offered sage advice about anger: "When angry, count to ten." Apparently, Thomas Jefferson improved on Mr. Franklin's advice and said, "When angry count to ten. When very angry, count to one hundred." After considering the advice of two of America's finest statesman, Mark Twain reportedly said, "When angry, count four; when very angry, swear!"

This account is probably apocryphal, but it does illustrate two strategies embraced by many. Some individuals are likely to deal with their anger through "control"; others are more likely to "vent" their frustration; and still others alternate between the two. Such conflicting phrases as "bite your tongue" and "get it out of your system" are common advice with respect to dealing with anger. While we are not as likely to observe those who attempt to control their anger, the public expression of anger is becoming common and is even encouraged by some. Elder Russell M. Nelson has stated:

> My concern is that contention is becoming accepted
> as a way of life. From what we see and hear in the media,
> the classroom, and the workplace, all are now infected to
> some degree with contention. How easy it is, yet how

wrong it is, to allow habits of contention to pervade matters of spiritual significance, because contention is forbidden by divine decree:

"The Lord God hath commanded that men should not murder; that they should not lie; that they should not steal; that they should not take the name of the Lord their God in vain; that they should not envy; that they should not have malice; that *they should not contend one with another*" (2 Ne. 26:32; emphasis added).[3]

While the primary purpose of the Book of Mormon is to "the convincing of the Jew and Gentile that Jesus is the Christ" (Title Page), its teachings also provide additional doctrinal clarity and counsel concerning anger. Elder Neal A. Maxwell stated: "In addition to the . . . confirmation of the Christocentricity of the universe, one sees numerous examples of elaboration and clarification of other basic and important truths in the Book of Mormon and the other books of scripture . . . These precious and plain truths are not mere footnotes. Instead, they are bolstering and guiding principles that can do so much to keep us mortals walking steadily on the strait and narrow path and from stumbling needlessly."[4]

An angel of the Lord taught the prophet Nephi that many parts of the gospel of Christ had been taken away to deceive the people and cause them to stumble. The angel said:

For behold, they have taken away from the gospel of the Lamb many parts which are plain and most precious;

and also many covenants of the Lord have they taken away.

And all this have they done that they might pervert the right ways of the Lord, that they might blind the eyes and harden the hearts of the children of men. . . .

. . . Because of the many plain and precious things which have been taken out of the book [the Bible], which were plain unto the understanding of the children of men . . . an exceedingly great many do stumble, yea, insomuch that Satan hath great power over them. (1 Nephi 13:26–29)

A most significant teaching in the Book of Mormon concerning anger is found in the teachings of Jesus Christ during His appearance in the Americas soon after His resurrection in Jerusalem. Note the differences between the text of the Sermon on the Mount found in the King James Version (KJV) of the Bible and the similar sermon at the temple given by the Savior during His visit to the inhabitants of ancient America:

Ye have heard that it was said by them of old time, Thou shalt not kill; and whosoever shall kill shall be in danger of the judgment:

But I say unto you, That whosoever is angry with his brother *without a cause* shall be in danger of the judgment: and whosoever shall say to his brother, Raca, shall be in danger of the council; but whosoever shall say, Thou fool, shall be in danger of hell fire. (Matthew 5:21–22; emphasis added)

Ye have heard that it hath been said by them of old time, and it is also written before you, that thou shalt not kill, and whosoever shall kill shall be in danger of the judgment of God;

But I say unto you, that whosoever is angry with his brother shall be in danger of his judgment. And whosoever shall say to his brother, Raca, shall be in danger of the council; and whoever shall say, Thou fool, shall be in danger of hell fire. (3 Nephi 12:21–22)

This comparison shows that the principal difference between the passage in the King James Version of the Bible and the corresponding passage in the Book of Mormon is that the latter does not contain the phrase "without a cause." The implication of this difference is significant: The biblical translation appears to provide justification for our anger; the Book of Mormon does not.

Interestingly, though the King James Version contains the phrase "without a cause," most other biblical translations do not. One scholar wrote that while there is not a "unanimous consensus" among the early manuscripts, many of the early Christian theologians such as Jerome, Tertullian, and Origen mention that the phrase "without a cause" was not found in the oldest manuscripts familiar to them.[5] Under inspiration, the Prophet Joseph Smith chose not to include the phrase "without a cause" in the Joseph Smith Translation of the Bible:

But I say unto you the *whosoever is angry with his brother, shall be in danger of his judgment;* and whosoever shall say to his brother, Raca, or Rabcha, shall be in danger of the council; and whosoever shall say to his brother, Thou fool, shall be in danger of hell fire. (JST Matthew 5:22)

Note various other translations of Matthew 5:22:

But I say to you that every one *who is angry with his brother shall be liable to judgment;* whoever insults his brother shall be liable to the council, and whoever says, "You fool!" shall be liable to the hell of fire. (Revised Standard Version of the Bible, or RSV; emphasis added)

But I say to you that every one *who is angry with his brother shall be guilty before the court;* and whoever shall say to his brother, "Raca," shall be guilty before the supreme court; and whoever shall say, "You fool," shall be guilty enough to go into the fiery hell of fire. (New American Standard Bible, or NASB; emphasis added)

But I tell you that anyone *who is angry with his brother will be subject to judgment.* Again, anyone who says to his brother, "Raca," is answerable to the Sanhedrin. But anyone who says, "You fool!" will be in danger of the fire of hell. (New International Version of the Bible, or NIV; emphasis added)

But what I tell you is this: *Anyone who nurses anger against his brother must be brought to justice.* Whoever calls his brother "good for nothing" deserves the sentence of the court; whoever calls him "fool" deserves hell-fire. (Revised English Bible, or REB; emphasis added)

But I say to you, *whoever is angry with his brother will be liable to judgment,* and whoever says to his brother, "Raqa," will be answerable to the Sanhedrin, and whoever says, "You fool," will be liable to fiery Gehenna. (New American Bible, or NAB; emphasis added)

But I say to you that *if you are angry with a brother or sister, you will be liable to judgment;* and if you insult a brother or sister, you will be liable to the council; and if you say, "You fool," You will be liable to the hell of fire. (New Revised Standard Version, or NRSV; emphasis added)

Of these differing Bible translations, only the King James Version contains wording that justifies anger. Even the Textus Receptus, the Greek manuscript on which the King James Version is based, does not include the Greek words for "without a cause."[6] The King James translators chose to follow a reading that is apparently a late scribal addition not found in the earliest manuscripts or the writings of the earliest Christians.

In addition to counsel against anger in 3 Nephi 12:22, the Savior also identifies the source of contention: "For verily, verily I say unto you, he that hath the spirit of contention is not of me, but is of the devil, who is the father of contention, and he stirreth up the hearts of men to contend with anger, one with another" (3 Nephi 11:29–30).

THE ANGER OF THE LORD

It is clear that the Book of Mormon contains strong teachings against anger, so how are we to understand the anger of such righteous men as Moroni or even of God Himself? (Alma 59:13; Helaman 13:11). We are led to ask, "Is there such an experience as righteous anger?" We might also ask, "What of the incidents in the scriptures where the Savior was angry—aren't we to follow his example?"

An analysis of the Bible shows that the Old Testament contains 375 instances in which God is described as showing anger.[7] The New Testament contains only one reference in which the word *anger* is used in connection with Jesus Christ:

> And he entered again into the synagogue; and there was a man there with a withered hand.
>
> And they [the Pharisees] watched him, whether he would heal him on the sabbath day; that they might accuse him.
>
> And he saith unto the man which had the withered hand, Stand forth.
>
> And he saith unto them, Is it lawful to do good on the sabbath days, or to do evil? to save life, or to kill? But they held their peace.
>
> And when he had looked round about on them with *anger, being grieved for the hardness of their hearts,* he saith

unto the man, Stretch forth thine hand. And he stretched it out: and his hand was restored whole as the other.

And the Pharisees went forth, and straightway took counsel with the Herodians against him, how they might destroy him. (Mark 3:1–6; emphasis added)[8]

From these verses, it is evident that the Savior's anger was a selfless concern not only for the man with the withered hand but also for the hard-hearted Pharisees. One thing we can learn from this account is that the Savior's anger is fundamentally different from the anger of the natural man. Almost everything the natural man does is calculated in some way to "serve the creature more than the Creator" (Romans 1:25). The Book of Mormon teaches that everything the Savior does is designed for the welfare and happiness of others. "He doeth not *anything* save it be for the benefit of the world; for he loveth the world, even that he layeth down his own life that he may draw all men unto him. Wherefore, he commandeth none that they shall not partake of his salvation" (2 Nephi 26:24; emphasis added).

The Book of Mormon also teaches us that the Savior's anger is a representation of His love for us. Justice is as much a quality of God's love as is His mercy:

Yea, and we may see at the very time when he doth prosper his people, yea, in the increase of their fields, their flocks and their herds, and in gold, and in silver, and in all manner of precious things of every kind and art; sparing their lives, and delivering them out of the hands of their enemies; softening the hearts of their enemies that they should not declare wars against them; yea, and in fine, *doing all things for the welfare and happiness of his people;* yea, then is the time that they do harden their hearts, and do forget the Lord their God, and do trample under their feet the Holy One—yea, and this because of their ease, and their exceedingly great prosperity.

And thus we see that *except the Lord doth chasten his people* with many afflictions, yea, except he doth visit them with death and with terror, and with famine and with all manner of pestilence, they will not remember him. (Helaman 12:2–3; emphasis added)

God wants nothing more than for us to remember Him and keep His commandments, for in doing so we enter into a covenant relationship with Him and will receive the blessings of heaven and earth. God's anger is much like His jealousy: both are expressions of His love as He seeks to assist us in becoming like Him. God's jealousy of our worship of other gods is not narcissistic in any way but is rather a plea that we remain free from the damning consequences of failing to worship Him. He declares:

Thou shalt not make unto thee any graven image, or any likeness of any thing that is in heaven above, or that is in the earth beneath, or that is in the water under the earth:

Thou shalt not bow down thyself to them, nor serve them: *for I the Lord thy God am a jealous God,* visiting the iniquity of the fathers upon the children unto the third and fourth generation of them that hate me;

And shewing mercy unto thousands of them that love me, and keep my commandments." (Exodus 20:4–6; emphasis added)

Anger is indeed a characteristic of God's perfection, but it is critical we come to a correct understanding of His selfless nature.

THE CLEANSING OF THE TEMPLE

Just as some of the people in the Book of Mormon sought "to excuse themselves in committing whoredoms, because of the things which were written" in the scriptures (Jacob 2:23), others today use various events in the Savior's life as justification for their anger. It has been my experience, both professionally and ecclesiastically, that the most common justification that Christians, including Latter-day Saints, give for their own selfish anger is the Savior's cleansing of the temple.

Most Bible scholars agree that the Savior cleansed the temple twice. The first cleansing is mentioned only by John; the second cleansing is described by Matthew, Mark, and Luke. As we read the following accounts of the cleansings, note that the words *anger* and *wrath* do not appear. Could it be that the Savior did what needed to be done without being angry?

Matthew's Account

And Jesus went into the Temple of God, and cast out all them that sold and bought in the temple, and overthrew the tables of the moneychangers, and the seats of them that sold doves,

And said unto them, It is written, My house shall be called the house of prayer; but ye have made it a den of thieves. (Matthew 21:12–13)

Matthew then described what the Savior did immediately after He cleansed the temple:

And the blind and the lame came to him in the temple; *and he healed them.* (Matthew 21:14; emphasis added)

It is highly unlikely that the Savior could have healed the afflicted had He just been through an angry, violent experience. President Brigham Young taught: "Do not be angry. . . . Do not get so angry you cannot pray: do not allow yourselves to become so angry that you cannot feed an enemy—even your worst enemy, if an opportunity should present itself."[9]

Mark's Account

And they come to Jerusalem: and Jesus went into the temple, and began to cast out them that sold and bought in the temple, and overthrew the tables of the money-changers, and the seats of them that sold doves;

And would not suffer that any man should carry any vessel through the temple.

And he taught, saying unto them, Is it not written, My house shall be called of all nations the house of prayer? but ye have made it a den of thieves. (Mark 11:15–17)

Sometimes we entangle ourselves in a false dichotomy, believing that our choice is between angrily doing what needs to be done and passively allowing what should not happen. We fail to recognize that we can confront, chastise, and reprove without being contentious.

Luke's Account

Luke's account is the most concise of the four. He wrote, simply:

> And he went into the temple, and began to cast out them that sold therein, and them that bought;
>
> Saying unto them, It is written, My house is the house of prayer: but ye have made it a den of thieves. (Luke 19:45–46)

John's Account

> And the Jews' passover was at hand, and Jesus went up to Jerusalem,
>
> And found in the temple those that sold oxen and sheep and doves, and the changers of money sitting:
>
> And when he had made a scourge of small cords, he drove them all out of the temple, and the sheep, and the oxen; and poured out the changers' money, and overthrew the tables;

And said unto them that sold doves, Take these things hence; make not my Father's house an house of merchandise. (John 2:13–16)

Although the Savior may have used physical force to cleanse the temple, it wasn't a selfish tirade like many of us have experienced. Compare the Savior's actions in the temple with those of an individual described by President David O. McKay:

> I learned through a letter of a condition which I think, so far as members of the Church are concerned, is absolutely inexcusable. A husband and wife quarreling—the husband demeaning himself to such an extent as to curse his wife, and *in a mad fit of anger overturning a table* spread with dishes—a creature in the form of a man harboring the nature of an animal! A man in such a mental state that the anger itself does him more harm than the condition which aroused his anger, and in reality, brothers and sisters, he suffers more from the vexation than he does from the acts that aroused that vexation.[10]

Such is not the personality of the Savior, nor should it be of any who seek to follow Him.

In the *Lectures on Faith* we learn that we must come to a "*correct* idea of [God's] character, perfections, and attributes" if we desire to truly exercise faith in him.[11] Selfish anger is not and never has been an attribute of God. The adversary is the master of counterfeit and will do his best to deceive us into confusing justice with vengeance.

JUSTICE MISINTERPRETED

The following story illustrates how God's justice is often mistakenly interpreted as anger or vengeance. Several years ago a member of the ward of which I was the bishop asked if I would interview him for a temple recommend. I was pleased when he told me that he thought it was time he got his life back in order by returning to the temple after an absence of some years. He informed me that his niece was being married in the temple in three weeks and he would like to be there with her and her family. Among the questions I asked him was a query about tithing. He explained that because of some financial problems, he had not been paying tithing but had managed to give a few dollars to a local charity. As we finished the interview, I told him I wouldn't be able to give him a recommend then but that I was willing to do all that I could to assist him to become worthy to receive one at a later time. My heart ached for him, but I felt that issuing him a temple recommend would only prolong his problems. He became enraged and told me that I was a terrible bishop, that I was mean and insensitive and too young and immature to make such judgments.

After dealing with his numerous protestations, I suggested he return home, assemble his financial records, and invite his wife to come with him to visit with me about their finances. I also volunteered the services of my counselor who was adept with numbers and budgets. After calming down, he accepted my invitation and went home to do as I had suggested. Later that evening the four of us were able to make good progress toward preparing both him and his wife to return to the temple. What a joyous occasion it was several months later when I issued temple recommends to them. He missed his niece's wedding, but his faith in Christ was greatly increased.

This man had initially interpreted my judgment of him as mean, insensitive, and punishing. But if I had succumbed to his demands and issued him a recommend inappropriately, he might have interpreted my indulgence as mercy. It is easy to misunderstand the doctrine of Christ and accept Satan's counterfeit in its place.

Note the similarities between this story and the counsel the prophet Lehi gave to Laman, Lemuel, and others concerning how Nephi had treated them: "And ye have murmured because he hath been plain unto you. Ye say that he hath used sharpness; ye say that he hath been angry with you; but behold, his sharpness was the sharpness of the power of the word of God, which was in him; and *that which ye call anger was the truth,* according to that which is in God, which he could not restrain, manifesting boldly concerning your iniquities" (2 Nephi 1:26; emphasis added).

This verse illustrates how it is possible for us to misinterpret the selfless *justice* of God as selfish anger and vengeance. This may be one reason some people perceive Jehovah as a merciless and vengeful ruler and not a kind and loving God, for "the guilty taketh the truth to be hard, for it cutteth them to the very center" (1 Nephi 16:2). Not once had I raised my voice, nor had I even felt any tinge of animosity toward this ward member. But he was initially convinced I was an unjust judge simply because my judgment did not agree with his.

Another segment of scripture that is often taken out of context to counterfeit a justification for anger is found in the Doctrine and Covenants where the Lord describes how at times leadership requires "reproving betimes with sharpness" (D&C 121:43). But note the verses that precede this verse: "No power or influence can or ought to be maintained by virtue of the priesthood, only by *persuasion,* by *long-suffering,* by *gentleness* and *meekness,* and by *love unfeigned;* by *kindness,* and pure knowledge, which shall greatly enlarge the soul without hypocrisy, and without guile" (D&C 121:41–42; emphasis added). We are also instructed to reprove another only "when moved upon by the Holy Ghost; and then showing forth afterwards an increase of love toward him whom thou hast reproved, lest he esteem thee to be his enemy" (D&C 121:43). The only context and grounding from which appropriate reproof can come is the genuine love and gentleness that these verses describe.[12]

In the New Testament, we read the Savior's invitation to "come, follow me" (Luke 18:22). If following the Savior means that we follow His example, then should we also seek to develop godlike anger? The answer to this question is both yes and no: *yes,* because there is such a quality as selfless, righteous anger; and *no,* because selfless anger can turn selfish in an instant and is incredibly easy to distort.

PHILOSOPHIES OF THE WORLD

Most philosophies concerning anger can be divided into two distinct camps: those who believe that anger is inevitable but in need of rational control, and those who believe that anger should be experienced and expressed (vented). Interestingly, these two competing philosophies have a scriptural connection. When the apostle Paul was first in the city of Athens awaiting the arrival of his missionary companions, he encountered two different groups of philosophers: the Stoics and the Epicureans (Acts 17:18). The Stoics believed that happiness came through the *control* of passion and indifference to external events; the Epicureans believed that happiness was to be found in the *expression* of passion and the experience of sensation. The gospel of Jesus Christ has some commonalities with both philosophies—"bridle all your passions, that ye may be filled with love" (Alma 38:12) and "men are, that they might have joy" (2 Nephi 2:25)—but there are ever-present counterfeits of self-righteousness and lustful expression or consumption (Mormon 9:28). Professor C. Terry Warner, one of my treasured colleagues at Brigham Young University, illustrates the first of these counterfeit philosophies in a story about a man he identifies as Philip:

> I planned, after an orderly dinner with no squabbling and no stern looks from me, to gather our two little children around the fireplace, read them a story, tuck them into bed, and tell them I loved them
>
> My train was an hour late. When I finally got home,

I went through the door determined to be cheerful and kind. But dinner wasn't on the table. Marsha wasn't even getting it ready. It was her turn to fix it, too. Was she waiting for *me* to do it?

For a moment I felt I ought to help her out. But then I just got bitter. How could I be the kind of father I'm supposed to be in this kind of mess?

I felt like letting out a bellow, but I didn't. I never do. I did what I always do. I hung up my coat (so there would be at least one thing put away in the house) and went to work cleaning up the mess. First, I put the children in the tub and got them properly bathed. Then I did the dishes and put away clothes and vacuumed everywhere.

Marsha said, "Please, stop, will you?" I'm sure she felt humiliated to have me pitch in when she had obviously been wasting time. People who don't act responsibly are going to feel humiliated by people who do.

But I didn't say anything back. Maybe I should have given her "what for" or not helped her at all. But I wasn't going to stoop to her level. And I tried not to have an angry expression, even though it was hard. I'm above pouting and tantrums and that sort of thing.

It took till ten o'clock. When we went to bed, Marsha was still upset. After all these years I know her well enough to say no matter how hard I had worked, she still wouldn't have appreciated it.[13]

From his outward actions, Philip was "doing" all the right

things and was in complete "control" of his anger. Philip's problems were not with his outward behavior, however, but with an inward, self-justifying mindset. The Savior describes individuals whose attitudes were similar to Philip's: "Woe unto you, scribes and Pharisees, hypocrites! for ye are like unto whited sepulchers, which indeed appear beautiful outward, but are within full of dead men's bones, and of all uncleanness. Even so ye also *outwardly appear righteous unto men, but within ye are full of hypocrisy and iniquity*" (Matthew 23:27–28; emphasis added). Philip had deceived himself into believing that his actions were virtuous examples of righteousness, but nothing could have been further from the truth. Such self-righteous "control" of anger is one of the greatest deceptions of our day. Self-righteous Latter-day Saints are no better than the Pharisees of old; in fact, we have the greater condemnation because we know better (D&C 82:3).

On the other hand, there are those who believe that the best way to deal with anger is to express it, or vent it. These individuals, whether they know it or not, are espousing a perspective initiated by the adversary and made famous by Sigmund Freud.[14] The words of popular author and lecturer John Bradshaw represent this perspective: "The reason we have so much abuse in our families is that we do not allow anger in our families. If rage can come out, it can spend itself and be done with. . . . It's not the hatred expressed that's the problem; it's the hatred swallowed."[15]

Dr. Bradshaw and others advocating this Freudian perspective would have Philip give up the stoic notion of "control" and adopt a more epicurean perspective and express, or vent, his anger. Individuals who vent their anger in this way often argue that they are simply being "honest about their feelings." The trouble with this justification is that it is possible to be *honest about a lie.* In other words, our "honesty" may be real but not authorized—much like a counterfeit coin. John the Revelator taught us that "if we say that we have no sin, we deceive ourselves" (1 John 1:8). Our deception may be that we have come to believe our own lie that our anger is justified and that it is actually caused by someone or something outside of our control. The Book of Mormon counters this philosophy by teaching that men and women are moral agents and are free "to act for themselves and *not be acted upon*" by their environment (2 Nephi 2:26; emphasis added).

If neither controlled suppression nor expression of anger is the answer, what are we to do? Again, the Book of Mormon provides some meaningful answers. In 4 Nephi we read, "And it came to pass that there was no contention in the land, *because of the love of God which did dwell in the hearts of the people*" (1:15; emphasis added). From this verse we learn that the love of God supplants selfish anger.

But two questions quickly follow: What is perfect love, and how do we obtain it? The prophet Mormon, using the word *charity,* described love as follows: "And charity *suffereth long, and is kind, and envieth not, and is not puffed up, seeketh not her own,* is *not easily provoked, thinketh no evil,* and rejoiceth not in iniquity but rejoiceth in the truth, beareth all things, believeth all things, hopeth all things, endureth all things" (Moroni 7:45;

emphasis added). From this description, we can see that the love of God is more than an act or an emotion; it is a state of being. We can do loving things and even feel loving feelings and yet not be a loving person; however, we cannot be a loving person without doing loving things. Perhaps this is what Mormon was describing when he wrote, "For behold, a bitter fountain cannot bring forth good water; neither can a good fountain bring forth bitter water" (Moroni 7:11).

The real answers to Philip's problems are not in what he did or didn't do when he first entered his home but in who he was as a person. Philip was doing a lot of "loving" things, such as cleaning up the house and bathing the kids, but his heart wasn't right, and his wife sensed it. He was a bitter fountain bringing forth bitter water. Though Philip could have made wiser choices that evening to correct what was happening, what he really needed was a power much greater than his own. Christian philosopher C. S. Lewis wrote:

> When I come to my evening prayers and try to reckon up the sins of the day, nine times out of ten the most obvious one is some sin against charity; I have sulked or snapped or sneered or snubbed or stormed. And the excuse that immediately springs to my mind is that the provocation was so sudden and unexpected: I was caught off my guard, I had not time to collect myself. . . . Surely what a man does when he is taken off his guard is the best evidence for what sort of man he is. Surely what pops out before the man has time to put on a

disguise is the truth. If there are rats in the cellar you are most likely to see them if you go in very suddenly. But the suddenness does not create the rats: it only prevents them from hiding. In the same way the suddenness of the provocation does not make me an ill-tempered man: it only shows me what an ill-tempered man I am. . . . Now that cellar is out of reach of my conscious will. I can to some extent control my acts: I have no direct control over my temperament. And if (as I said before) what we are matters even more than what we do—if, indeed, what we do matters chiefly as evidence of what we are—then it follows that the change which I most need to undergo is a change that my own direct, voluntary efforts cannot bring about. And this applies to my good actions too. How many of them were done for the right motive? . . . But I cannot, by direct moral effort, give myself new motives. After the first few steps in the Christian life we realise that everything which really needs to be done in our souls can be done only by God.[16]

Even though there is much we can do to eliminate selfish anger from our lives, if we don't continually look to the Savior and His atonement, we will fail. On the other hand, if we will day after day, month after month, and year after year, nurture our faith in Christ, repent of our sins, keep our covenants, and follow the promptings of the Holy Ghost, we will experience a change of heart and be filled with the gift of love. Mormon wrote: "And the remission of sins bringeth meekness, and lowliness of heart; and because of meekness and lowliness of heart cometh the visitation of the Holy Ghost, which Comforter fil-leth with hope and perfect love, which love endureth by dili-gence unto prayer, until the end shall come, when all the saints shall dwell with God" (Moroni 8:26). Mormon also invited us to "pray unto the Father with all the energy of heart, that ye may be filled with this love, which he hath bestowed upon all who are true followers of his Son, Jesus Christ" (Moroni 7:48).

I have often wondered what Philip's response to his wife would have been if his heart had been right. A more important question is to consider how we respond when we are faced with similar situations. Are there rats in our cellars?

The Lord asks us to repent of unrighteous feelings as well as ungodly thoughts and actions, and by doing so we are "born of God" (Mosiah 27:28). The prophet Nephi taught us of his experiences with anger:

> And why should I yield to sin, because of my flesh?
> Yea, why should I give way to temptations, that the evil
> one have place in my heart to destroy my peace and afflict
> my soul? *Why am I angry because of mine enemy?*
>
> Awake, my soul! No longer droop in sin. Rejoice, O
> my heart, and give place no more for the enemy of my
> soul.
>
> *Do not anger again because of mine enemies.* . . .
>
> O Lord, *Wilt thou redeem my soul?* Wilt thou deliver
> me out of the hands of mine enemies? Wilt thou make
> me that I may shake at the appearance of sin? . . .
>
> O Lord, I have trusted in thee, and *I will trust in thee*

forever. I will not put my trust in the arm of flesh. (2 Nephi 4:27–34; emphasis added)

Nephi came to understand that he could no longer use the sins of others as justification for his own. He also recognized that he could not be free of his own sins by trusting in himself or in the theories of man but that he must seek to have his anger replaced by love through the atonement of Christ.

Several years ago, a dear friend shared with me his personal struggle with anger and how, through Christ, he learned to overcome it:

> I had grown up in the Church, served a successful mission, and believed in the gospel. But somehow I never felt the happiness I had always sought. I married but soon found my unhappiness to go in cycles as I would make the effort to pray and be obedient but then would quit seeking divine help. Too many times I tried to rely on my own strength and knowledge to work out life's problems.
>
> I found myself during these times becoming intolerant of the mistakes of others and angry when my agenda was not met. At times I would attempt to control my family by silence and withholding affection. Eventually this pattern of living and contention led to physical confrontations with my wife. Sometimes I would become angry without warning to insignificant provocations. I would then feel awful and go through the repentance process and resolve to do better. But why did it not stick?
>
> Gradually the same patterns came back. My wife and

I went to many counselors, seeking help with our marriage relationship. We were taught to communicate more effectively, we found out why we behaved in certain ways because of our gender, and we learned skills to cope with stress and outside influences. "Change your behavior," I was told time after time. But nothing seemed to change; our relationship became worse and ended in divorce. The pain was immense. I didn't understand what to do, or how to change.

Luckily for me, a loving bishop took me under his wing. I truly felt his love for me, which softened my heart to his counsel. He pointed me to the Atonement and helped me understand that only Jesus Christ could bring about the change I searched for.

I believed his words and began searching and learning about the Atonement. Most of my adult life I had believed in Christ, but I had never believed that his promises were for me. As I began understanding what the Atonement was all about, my heart changed.

I no longer had desires to choose evil but to choose good in my life. I found myself pouring out my soul to my God in prayer many times throughout the day, asking that my faith in Christ would increase and that my heart would be filled with love. I found that the more I sought after him, the more I could feel his love and assurance.

Day by day my faith increases. I have hope in those wonderful promises that I see all through the scriptures. I

have found great peace because of the love I feel for my
Father in Heaven.

The best part of all of this is the desires I have to love
those around me. There is peace in my home. My relationship with my children has reached new levels, and I
look for opportunities to serve and help others.[17]

"Can ye be angry, and not sin?" is from Joseph Smith's
translation of Ephesians 4:26. The complete verse reads, "Can
ye be angry, and not sin? let not the sun go down upon your
wrath." The King James Version reads, "Be ye angry, and sin
not: let not the sun go down upon your wrath" (KJV Ephesians
4:26). The clarification from the Joseph Smith Translation does
not categorically define all anger as sin, but it does call it into
question. Just as our thoughts, words, and deeds can be righteous or wicked, so can our emotions be righteous or wicked,
as well.

Anger can be the expression of a godly attribute, but most
often it is evidence of our unwillingness and inability to keep
the greatest of all the commandments: to love God and to love
our neighbor (Matthew 22:36–40). Anger also places us in
jeopardy of the judgment of others as well as of God. Though
the Bible seemingly provides justification for angry feelings, the
Book of Mormon does not. It teaches us that selfish feelings of
anger and acts of contention are tools of the adversary.

Selfless anger is an attribute of God's personality and is an
expression of His love. But selfish anger is a characteristic of
the natural man and an expression of selfishness. The Book of

Mormon teaches that the only way we can adequately address our anger is through the atonement of Christ. King Benjamin taught: "For the natural man is an enemy to God, and has been from the fall of Adam, and will be, forever and ever, unless he yields to the enticings of the Holy Spirit, and putteth off the natural man and becometh a saint through the atonement of Christ the Lord, and becometh as a child, submissive, meek, humble, patient, full of love, willing to submit to all things which the Lord seeth fit to inflict upon him, even as a child doth submit to his father" (Mosiah 3:19).

How very blessed we are to have the teachings of prophets, both ancient and modern, to help clarify and support us in "the confounding of false doctrines and laying down of contentions, and establishing peace" (2 Nephi 3:12).

CHAPTER FOUR

Is Divorce the Answer to a Faltering Marriage?

In September 1995, President Gordon B. Hinckley introduced "The Family: A Proclamation to the World": "We, the First Presidency and the Council of the Twelve Apostles of The Church of Jesus Christ of Latter-day Saints, solemnly proclaim that marriage between a man and a woman is ordained of God and that the family is central to the Creator's plan for the eternal destiny of His children."[1]

Clearly, marriage and family relationships are vital in Latter-day Saint theology and practice. Yet some in the world have argued that the family is detrimental to the progress of the individual. Social historians Steven Mintz and Susan Kellogg observed:

> In the early 1960s, marriage and family ties were regarded by the "human potential movement" as potential threats to individual fulfillment as a man or a woman. The highest forms of human needs, contended proponents of the new psychologies, were autonomy, independence,

growth, and creativity, all of which could be thwarted by "existing relationships and interactions." [2]

Such a philosophy, sometimes called *individualism,* underlies much of our present-day culture. It has been identified by our prophets as a major contributor to many of the problems undermining today's families. This cultural shift from an emphasis on family to a focus on self has had a significant effect on the numbers of couples divorcing and the accompanying increase in single-parent families. Men and women have been influenced to be more concerned with their own growth than with nurturing their spouses and children.

The adversary's deceptive emphasis on individualism also explains to some degree the decrease in the number of children born to married couples and the increase in the number of children born to single mothers. Other consequences of this focus on self include an increase in cohabitation (living together without being married), a decrease in the numbers of those who marry, and an increase in abortion and occurrences of abuse. [3]

Although the rates at which these various problems occur appear to have remained the same during the past several years, they are nonetheless not acceptable and continue to be a serious concern. Perhaps these problems are a part of the reason why our prophets, seers, and revelators, our watchmen "upon the tower" (D&C 101:45), have provided strong counsel concerning the family. President Gordon B. Hinckley has stated:

Perhaps our greatest concern is with families. The family is falling apart all over the world. The old ties that bound together father and mother and children are breaking everywhere. We must face this in our own midst. There are too many broken homes among our own. The love that led to marriage somehow evaporates, and hatred fills its place. Hearts are broken, children weep. Can we not do better? Of course, we can. It is self-ishness that brings about most of these tragedies. If there is forbearance, if there is forgiveness, if there is an anxious looking after the happiness of one's companion, then love will flourish and blossom.[4]

It is true that many of the consequences of selfish individu-alism can be found among Latter-day Saint families, but there is also strong evidence that living the gospel makes a positive difference. Contrary to popular opinion, the divorce rate among faithful Latter-day Saints is much lower than the national average.[5] Although there is some indication that the divorce rate among Latter-day Saints may have increased dur-ing the past several years, formal research indicates that just under 6 percent of men and women who have been sealed in the temple obtain a civil divorce.[6] The divorce rate for Latter-day Saints who marry outside the temple is five times higher than for those who are sealed in the temple. These statistics are relatively good news for Church members in general, but for the families who experience it, divorce is tragic. Never should we congratulate ourselves for the success of the ninety and nine while the one is suffering (Matthew 18:12). Perhaps paradoxically, the doctrine of eternal marriage and family provides scriptural and prophetic counsel and comfort to those whose family relationships are at present less than ideal.

THE IDEAL FAMILY

Unlike any other faith of which I am aware, The Church of Jesus Christ of Latter-day Saints proclaims that through Christ and the ordinances of His priesthood, marriage and family relationships may be eternal. Second only to our worship of God and our reliance upon the merits, mercy, and grace of Jesus Christ, Latter-day Saints believe that family relationships should be at the center of our lives. The family is not only the most important *means* by which our Heavenly Father prepares us to once again enter His presence but also the most important *end,* for the family is intended to be eternal. Elder Richard G. Scott commented on the importance of striving for the ideal family and some of the challenges and blessings that accompany this desire:

> Throughout your life on earth, seek diligently to fulfill the fundamental purposes of this life *through the ideal family.* While you may not have yet reached that ideal, do all you can through obedience and faith in the Lord to consistently draw as close to it as you are able. Let nothing dissuade you from that objective. If it requires fundamental changes in your personal life, make them. . . . If you have lost the vision of eternal marriage, rekindle it.

If your dream requires patience, give it. . . . Don't become overanxious. Do the best you can. We cannot say whether that blessing will be obtained on this side of the veil or beyond it, but the Lord will keep His promises. In His infinite wisdom, He will make possible all you qualify in worthiness to receive. Do not be discouraged. Living a pattern of life as close as possible to the ideal will provide much happiness, great satisfaction, and impressive growth while here on earth regardless of your current life circumstances.[7]

Striving for the "ideal family" can be challenging and is often discouraging for most of us. It is important to remember that in mortality the family may not be perfect, but as a family strives for the ideal established by the Savior, that family can one day become perfect and eternal. Consider the story Rabbi Lehrman has told of a young boy who "walks into an office building and sees a clock too high on the wall for anyone to reach. To adjust the time, workmen must climb a tall ladder. The boy asks his father, 'Why is the clock set so high, where nobody can reach it?' 'It's simple,' answers the father. 'The clock used to be lower, within reach of everybody. People would pass by, look at their watch, and adjust the clock to match their watch. When they moved the clock higher, people would look at it and adjust their watches accordingly.' "[8]

The same principle is true in discussing doctrines related to marriage and the family. There are no perfect families, but we as individuals and families must strive to live up to the high standards that have been set by the Lord and His servants.

Without these standards, most people would simply do "what is right in their own eyes" (Judges 21:25) and miss the blessings the Lord has in store for us if we are obedient to His counsel.

JESUS AND DIVORCE

The New Testament contains an important account of Jesus Christ being asked about the legitimacy of divorce. The Pharisees, a group among the Jews who took pride in their strict observance of the law of Moses, asked the Savior, "Is it lawful for a man to put away [divorce] his wife for every cause?" (Matthew 19:3).

It appears that these Pharisees were attempting to trap the Savior into offending one or another of the groups of Jews present. If Jesus answered that divorce was allowed only if the spouse was guilty of sexual sin, He would offend the followers of Rabbi Hillel (60 B.C.–A.D. 9), who taught that a man should be allowed to divorce for many reasons, including loss of interest, a more attractive woman, or even his wife's poor cooking. On the other hand, if Jesus responded that a man could divorce his wife for "every cause," he would offend the followers of Rabbi Shammi (50 B.C.–A.D. 30), who taught that divorce should be rare and for very limited reasons.[9]

Jesus answered the Pharisees by teaching them the doctrine of eternal marriage:

> And he answered and said unto them, Have ye not read, that he which made them at the beginning made them male and female,

> And said, For this cause shall a man leave father and mother, and shall cleave to his wife: and they twain shall be one flesh?
>
> Wherefore they are no more twain, but one flesh. What therefore God hath joined together, let not man put asunder. (Matthew 19:4–6)

The Pharisees responded by citing the teachings of Moses that permitted divorce in a given circumstance: "Why did Moses then command to give a writing of divorcement, and to put her away?" (Matthew 19:7). Jesus countered by providing the following instruction:

> He saith unto them, Moses because of the hardness of your hearts suffered you to put away your wives: but from the beginning it was not so.
>
> And I say unto you, Whosoever shall put away his wife, except it be for fornication, and shall marry another, committeth adultery: and whoso marrieth her which is put away doth commit adultery. (Matthew 19:8–9)

Not only did Jesus declare the doctrine that marriage is intended to be eternal but He also taught a higher law pertaining to divorce.

LATTER-DAY PROPHETS AND DIVORCE

Even though we as Latter-day Saints are not currently bound by the higher law concerning divorce, the words of Jesus remind us of the high value the Lord and His servants place upon the marital relationship. Elder Bruce R. McConkie taught:

> Divorce is not part of the gospel plan no matter what kind of marriage is involved. But because men in practice do not always live in harmony with gospel standards, the Lord permits divorce for one reason or another, depending upon the spiritual stability of the people involved. In ancient Israel men had power to divorce their wives for relatively insignificant reasons. (Deut. 24:1–4.) Under the most perfect conditions there would be no divorce permitted except where sex sin was involved. In this day divorces are permitted in accordance with civil statutes, and the divorced persons are permitted by the Church to marry again without the stain of immorality which under a higher system would attend such a course.[10]

President David O. McKay taught that "Christ's ideal pertaining to marriage is the unbroken home." Still, he said, "there may be circumstances which make the continuance of the marriage state a greater evil than divorce. But these are extreme cases."[11]

Elder James E. Faust provided further clarification on what conditions might justify divorce:

> The importance of this subject emboldens me to say a word about covenant breaking. It must be recognized that some marriages just fail. To those in that circumstance, I extend understanding because every divorce

carries heartache with it. I hope what I say will not be disturbing. . . . The family relationship of father, mother, and child is the oldest and most enduring institution in the world. It has survived vast differences of geography and culture. This is because marriage between man and woman is a natural state and is ordained of God. It is a moral imperative. Those marriages performed in our temples, meant to be eternal relationships, then, become the most sacred covenants we can make. The sealing power given by God through Elijah is thus invoked, and God becomes a party to the promises.

What, then, might be "just cause" for breaking the covenants of marriage? Over a lifetime of dealing with human problems, I have struggled to understand what might be considered "just cause" for breaking of covenants. I confess I do not claim the wisdom or authority to definitively state what is "just cause." Only the parties to the marriage can determine this. They must bear the responsibility for the train of consequences which inevitably follow if these covenants are not honored. In my opinion, "just cause" should be nothing less serious than a prolonged and apparently irredeemable relationship which is destructive of a person's dignity as a human being.

At the same time, I have strong feelings about what is not provocation for breaking the sacred covenants of marriage. Surely it is not simply "mental distress," nor "personality differences," nor having "grown apart," nor having "fallen out of love." This is especially so where there are children. Enduring divine counsel comes from Paul: "Husbands, love your wives, even as Christ also loved the church, and gave himself for it." (Eph. 5:25.)[12]

President Gordon B. Hinckley has counseled: "The remedy for most marriage stress is not in divorce. It is in repentance. It is not in separation. It is in simple integrity." He continued: "There may be now and again a legitimate cause for divorce. I am not one to say that it is never justified. But I say without hesitation that this plague among us, which seems to be growing everywhere, is not of God, but rather is the work of the adversary of righteousness and peace and truth."[13]

THE DOCTRINE OF ETERNAL MARRIAGE

The apostle Paul taught: "Nevertheless neither is the man without the woman, neither the woman without the man, in the Lord" (1 Corinthians 11:11). Such a statement is representative of the significance of marriage and family relationships in ancient times as well as in the latter days. It is the doctrine of the Church that a man and a woman must be sealed in the holy temple for their marriage to be valid for eternity:

> Therefore, if a man marry him a wife in the world, and he marry her not by me nor by my word, and he covenant with her so long as he is in the world and she with him, their covenant and marriage are not of force when they are dead, and when they are out of the world; therefore, they are not bound by any law when they are out of the world.

109

Therefore, when they are out of the world they neither marry nor are given in marriage; but are appointed angels in heaven, which angels are ministering servants, to minister for those who are worthy of a far more, and an exceeding, and an eternal weight of glory.

For these angels did not abide my law; therefore, they cannot be enlarged, but remain separately and singly, without exaltation, in their saved condition, to all eternity; and from henceforth are not gods, but are angels of God forever and ever. (D&C 132:15–17)

These verses of latter-day scripture also help clarify the answer to the question some have concerning the words of Jesus to the Jewish Sadducees: "For in the resurrection they neither marry, nor are given in marriage, but are as the angels of God in heaven" (Matthew 22:30). It is understandable why this verse is interpreted by some to mean that marriage does not exist in the next world, because in one sense that interpretation is completely accurate. Revelation from the Lord to the Prophet Joseph Smith clearly explains that marriage will not exist in heaven for those (like the Sadducees to whom Jesus was speaking) who "marry . . . not by me nor by my word" (D&C 132:15). Clearly, those who have not been sealed in the holy temple, "when they are out of the world they neither marry nor are given in marriage; but are appointed angels in heaven" (D&C 132:16).

Of course, provision will be made for those who have not had the opportunity to be sealed in mortality. President Joseph

Fielding Smith commented on the specific example of women who do not have the opportunity of marrying in mortality:

> You good sisters, who are single and alone, do not fear, do not feel that blessings are going to be withheld from you. You are not under any obligation or necessity of accepting some proposal that comes to you which is distasteful for fear you will come under condemnation. If in your hearts you feel that the gospel is true, and would under proper conditions receive these ordinances and sealing blessings in the temple of the Lord; and that is your faith and your hope and your desire, and that does not come to you now; the Lord will make it up, and you shall be blessed—for *no blessing shall be withheld.* The Lord will judge you according to the desires of your hearts when blessings are withheld in this life, and he is not going to condemn you for that which you cannot help.[14]

THE PROMISE OF RECONCILIATION

"Whatever Jesus lays his hands upon lives. If Jesus lays his hands upon a marriage, it lives. If he is allowed to lay his hands on the family, it lives."[15] In these words President Howard W. Hunter reminded us that Jesus Christ is the *Savior* of the world and that His infinite atonement extends to every aspect of our lives, including our marriages and families. Not only can the atonement of Christ reconcile humans to God but also husband to wife, parent to child, and sibling to sibling. Such tools as "effective communication," "realistic expectations," and "developing similar goals and interests" can help in strengthening relationships and solving problems that arise in marriages and families, but the foundation upon which a marriage and family must be built is Jesus Christ. All other foundations will eventually fail. The Savior taught the ancient Nephites, "But if it be not built upon my gospel, and is built upon the works of men, or upon the works of the devil, verily I say unto you they have joy in their works for a season, and by and by the end cometh, and they are hewn down and cast into the fire, from whence there is no return" (3 Nephi 27:11).

From time to time in my role as a stake president, I work with couples whose marriages are falling down around them. These couples are usually suffering and are looking at divorce as a solution that will take the pain away and make life easier. By the time they have tried to work through their problems on their own, counseled with their bishops, had some contact with a therapist, and have then been referred on to me, divorce has become a serious option for one or both parties.

Some time ago I counseled with a sister whose faltering marriage had led to suicidal thoughts and feelings. Her husband had announced his intent to divorce her, and even though she had several children who would then need her more than ever before, the adversary had deceived her into believing that her family would be better off without her. Despite the efforts of many to help, her thoughts of taking her own life became more serious by the day, and she devised a plan by which she would end her life. Not only was this sister's marriage in question but her very life was in jeopardy as well.

Much to this sister's credit, she reached out for help. Feeling that her family and friends would be disappointed in her and being unable to contact her bishop, she called her stake president for help. After talking with her at length, providing counsel, and making the necessary arrangements to ensure that she wouldn't end her life, I also attempted to counsel with her husband, only to find him resistant to any attempts of reconciliation.

The sister's bishop, faithful friends, visiting teachers, and a trusted counselor did most of the day-to-day work with her in the weeks and months that followed; I continued to be in regular contact with her as well. One week from the time she first called me, I had set an appointment to meet her in my office at the stake center. I scheduled a couple of hours, anticipating that this session would go like the many I had experienced before and would take some time to effectively address the multitude of issues involved. As I went into the waiting room to greet her, I was astounded. No longer did she look as I had seen her the week before, nor as I had expected she would appear on this occasion. She radiated a strength and a peace that I hadn't foreseen. I quickly concluded to myself that her husband must have returned and they were in the process of reconciling their differences.

After we were seated in my office, I asked (confidant that I knew the answer), "Has your husband returned?"

"No," she said.

Not only had her husband not returned but the situation was probably worse than it had been the previous week. She told me that even though there didn't seem to be much hope for her marriage, she was feeling much better. She also said that she continued to feel the deep hurt she had described earlier but she no longer had suicidal feelings. She could sense that though she had a long road ahead of her, in the end everything would be okay.

After discussing some of the details of what was happening between her, her husband, and the children, I asked her to explain to me how it was that she was apparently doing so well in the face of very difficult circumstances. Was she being honest about how she felt? Was she masking what was really happening? Was she in denial? She responded by explaining that even though she hadn't analyzed why she was doing so much better, she had been reading the words of the prophets and had found a verse of scripture in the Book of Mormon that helped her explain her great hope. We read together the words of Helaman to his sons Nephi and Lehi:

> And now, my sons, remember, remember that it is upon the rock of our Redeemer, who is Christ, the Son of God, that ye must build your foundation; that when the devil shall send forth his mighty winds, yea, his shafts in the whirlwind, yea, when all his hail and his mighty storm shall beat upon you, it shall have no power over you to drag you down to the gulf of misery and endless wo, because of the rock upon which ye are built, which

is a sure foundation, a foundation whereon if men build they cannot fall. (Helaman 5:12)

Before this woman's marriage, the Savior had been the foundation of her life, but with the consuming responsibilities of marriage and motherhood, she had slowly shifted from being founded on Jesus Christ to being based on her husband and family. With her husband's announcement that he intended to divorce her and take the children with him, her foundation gave way, and she began what she described as a "free fall" into a hellish existence of suicidal thoughts and feelings and self-destructive behavior. It made my heart hurt to see this dear woman in such pain and to see the marriage eventually end, but what a joy it was to see a miracle begin to unfold as she came to remember the proper place of the Savior in her life.

It is a tragedy that many couples divorce who could have built strong and happy marriages if they had given their relationships time to heal. A recent research study indicated that 86 percent of unhappy couples who stayed together despite their marital problems reported that within five years, their marriages were much happier and they were pleased that they had not divorced.[16]

It is also important to note that for the most part, individuals who divorce and remarry report their second marriages to be no happier than their first.[17] Although there are certainly exceptions, a change of partners is not generally the best solution to a failing marriage. The prophet Moroni taught, "He that is happy shall be happy still, and he that is unhappy shall be unhappy still" (Mormon 9:14). Even though Moroni was describing the state of those who die and go on to the next world, his counsel has direct application to marriage as well. Happiness is more a matter of what is in our hearts than what our external circumstances may be.

Oftentimes individuals who decide upon divorce have come to believe the idea that if they aren't happy in their marriage, they and their children are better off if there is a divorce. This lie has Lucifer's lip prints all over it. As important as happiness is, it is false to believe that it should be our highest priority. The Prophet Joseph Smith taught that "happiness is the object and design of our existence; and will be the end thereof, if we pursue the path that leads to it; and this path is virtue, uprightness, faithfulness, holiness, and keeping all the commandments of God."[18] Happiness is certainly our Heavenly Father's "object and design" as He seeks our "immortality and eternal life" (Moses 1:39), but worshiping Him and following His will for us are the path we pursue. Happiness will come as a fruit of our relationship with God and our obedience to His will, but it is not intended to be the central focus of our lives.

The most important question for a person considering divorce is not "Am I happy?" or "Will divorcing my spouse make me happy?" but "What would God have me do?" Happiness can become a false god just as readily as most of the other forms of idolatry we pursue. Lehi's statement to his son Jacob, "For it must needs be, that there is an opposition in all things" (2 Nephi 2:11) includes marriage and family relation-ships as well. The doctrine of the fall of Adam and Eve as well as the doctrine of opposition are part of what distinguishes Latter-day Saint theology from the beliefs and practices of most other faiths. To believe that life should be constantly blissful is to misunderstand the restored gospel of Jesus Christ, especially as it is taught in the Book of Mormon. Elder Boyd K. Packer once taught:

> We are indoctrinated that somehow we should always be instantly emotionally comfortable. When that is not so, some become anxious—and all too frequently seek relief from counseling, from analysis, and even from medication.
>
> It was meant to be that life would be a challenge. To suffer some anxiety, some depression, some disappoint-ment, even some failure is normal.
>
> Teach our members that if they have a good, miser-able day once in a while, or several in a row, to stand steady and face them. Things will straighten out. There is great purpose in our struggle in life.[19]

It is more than coincidence that the Book of Mormon begins with a story about a family facing one crisis after another. Did the great prophet Lehi and his wife, Sariah, ever have any marital challenges? (1 Nephi 5). Did Sariah ever complain, and did Lehi ever murmur? (1 Nephi 5; 16). Did they ever have any problems with their children? (1 Nephi 1–2 Nephi 4). The answers to these questions make it clear that even the best of families face opposition. It is important to remember that we cannot experience joy without first becoming acquainted with sorrow. "Adam *fell* that men might be; and men are that they might have *joy*" (2 Nephi 2:25; emphasis added).

RESEARCH EVIDENCE ON MARRIAGE AND DIVORCE

Research confirms the words of prophets that even a marriage that is not blissful is better than divorce—especially for the children. As Elder Boyd K. Packer once stated, "Even a rickety marriage will serve good purpose as long as two people struggle to keep it from falling down around them."[20] In their book *The Case For Marriage: Why Married People Are Happier, Healthier, and Better Off Financially*, Professor Linda J. Waite and writer Maggie Gallagher summarize the research literature strongly supporting marriage and family relationships. The following is a brief summary of their findings concerning the influence of divorce on children:

Children raised in single-parent households are, on average, more likely to be poor, to have health problems and psychological disorders, to commit crimes and exhibit other conduct disorders, have somewhat poorer relationships with both family and peers, and as adults eventually get fewer years of education and enjoy less stable marriages and lower occupational statuses than children whose parents got and stayed married."[21]

This does not mean that children of divorced parents are destined for failure, especially if they are committed to the Savior and His teachings, but it may provide some understanding of why the Lord states that He "hateth" divorce (Malachi 2:16). Studies also support my own experience as a Church leader and as a trained psychologist that children living in single-parent families and in families where there are stepparents and stepchildren are much more likely to be the victims of domestic violence and sexual abuse.[22]

The negative influence of divorce on children appears to continue from one generation to the next. Children of divorced parents are more likely to be in unhappy marriages themselves and are also more likely to divorce than children from intact families.[23] While remembering that divorce can be a blessing in some circumstances, we can see that these findings represent the truth taught by the Lord to the prophet Moses that the sins and iniquities of the fathers would be visited "upon the children unto the third and fourth generation" (Exodus 20:5).

Research findings are also clear concerning the influence of the marital relationship itself. Being married is better for individuals physically, emotionally, spiritually, and financially than being divorced or single. People who are married have a longer life expectancy and are happier and more successful than those who are single or divorced. We are reminded that the Lord taught Moses, "It is not good that the man [or woman] should be alone" (Genesis 2:18).

Research indicates that although there are fewer incidents

of divorce, cohabitation, and abortion among faithful Latter-day Saints, in many ways we mirror the world. We continue to be viewed by the world as a "peculiar people" (1 Peter 2:9), but the contrast between the lives of Latter-day Saints and the world is not as great as it has been in years past. President Gordon B. Hinckley provided a warning as well as a cure for the challenges faced by Latter-day Saint families:

> I lift a warning voice to our people. We have moved too far toward the mainstream of society in this matter. Now, of course there are good families. There are good families everywhere. But there are too many who are in trouble. This is a malady with a cure. The prescription is simple and wonderfully effective. It is love. It is plain, simple, everyday love and respect. It is a tender plant that needs nurturing. But it is worth all of the effort we can put into it.[24]

The prophet Mormon provided two keys for how we can obtain the love President Hinckley described:

> Wherefore, my beloved brethren, pray unto the Father with all the energy of heart, that ye may be filled with this love, which he hath bestowed upon all who are true followers of his Son, Jesus Christ; that ye may become the sons of God; that when he shall appear we shall be like him, for we shall see him as he is; that we may have this hope; that we may be purified even as he is pure. Amen. (Moroni 7:48)

Not only is prayer a means of obtaining this gift of love but, as this verse reveals, this love is also bestowed upon those who are true followers of Christ. Our relationship with our Heavenly Father and Jesus Christ holds the keys to our earthly relationships with our families and others. Loving God by putting Him first in our lives is the only way we can truly love our neighbor. Elder Henry B. Eyring has wisely counseled:

> Keeping the first commandment [love the Lord thy God] always leads to keeping the second [love thy neighbour], because to love the Father and the Son is to serve those They love. In answer to our prayers for guidance, They send the Holy Ghost to tell us how to help others and to feel at least a part of God's love. So in that service, our love of God increases and the keeping of the second great commandment leads us back to the first, in an ascending circle.[25]

It has been my experience that too many marriages end in divorce that could have been saved if the marriage partners had better understood the Savior's teachings and allowed Him to heal their wounded relationships. One of the meanings of the word *atonement* (at-one-ment) is "reconciliation."[26] This at-one-ment has the power to help divided couples and families be "one" again. Although there are an infinite number of ways the atonement of Christ may be applied to a faltering marriage, perhaps the most important application is that of the Savior taking upon Himself our sins and sicknesses, thus allowing us to have the gift of the Holy Ghost fully operative in our lives.

The sanctifying influence of the Holy Ghost cleanses our souls and guides us in our marriage and family relationships in this life as well as preparing us for the life to come.

The doctrines related to marriage and family set a high standard for each of us to live. But as with each of the commandments given to us by the Lord, we know "that the Lord giveth no commandments unto the children of men, save he shall prepare a way for them that they may accomplish the thing which he commandeth them" (1 Nephi 3:7). We also can be assured "it is by grace that we are saved, after all we can do" (2 Nephi 25:23). The grace of the Lord Jesus Christ is eternally available to us and to our families. The only way we can fulfill the measure and purpose of our marriages and families is to be in a covenant relationship with God and for Him to bestow His blessings upon us.

At the time of our birth, each of us took upon ourselves a family name, and we became a Farnsworth, Sullivan, Rogers, Smith, or Glazier, and so forth. When a woman marries, she takes upon herself her husband's name, a symbol of the patriarchal partnership. As important as these names are, the most important name we take upon ourselves is the name of Christ when we are baptized, "for there is none other name under heaven given among men, whereby we must be saved" (Acts 4:12). It is only in first taking upon ourselves the name of Christ and becoming "the children of Christ, his sons, and his daughters" (Mosiah 5:7) that we can truly fulfill our divine destiny as families.

CHAPTER FIVE

Is Homosexuality a Sin or a Biological Fact?

One of the most difficult challenges Latter-day Saint families can face is for family members to reveal that they believe themselves to be gay or lesbian. Parents, siblings, and others are often anxious to know what the Church's position is on same-sex attraction and what they can do to assist their loved one. In the October 1998 general conference, President Gordon B. Hinckley responded to the question about the Church's attitude toward those who identify themselves as homosexual:

> My response is that we love them as sons and daughters of God. They may have certain inclinations which are powerful and which may be difficult to control. Most people have inclinations of one kind or another at various times. If they do not act upon these inclinations, then they can go forward as do all other members of the Church. If they violate the law of chastity and the moral

standards of the Church, then they are subject to the discipline of the Church, just as others are.

We want to help these people, to strengthen them, to assist them with their problems and to help them with their difficulties. But we cannot stand idle if they indulge in immoral activity, if they try to uphold and defend and live in a so-called same-sex marriage situation. To permit such would be to make light of the very serious and sacred foundation of God-sanctioned marriage and its very purpose, the rearing of families.[1]

Other hard questions asked by those confronted with the issue of homosexuality generally include whether homosexuality is a freewill choice an individual makes, an attraction influenced by such environmental factors as how the person was raised, or a biological fact. Probably the most important question asked is whether individuals who are attracted to someone of the same gender can be helped to change their sexual orientation. Individuals, families, and others who are faced with such a challenge can be helped by the words of latter-day prophets on the subject. Scriptural commentary and recent research also suggest ways that family, friends, and interested others can best respond to the difficult issue of same-sex attraction.

A LETTER FROM DAVID

Not long ago a family with whom I am acquainted received the following letter from their son (I have changed some of the details to protect the privacy of those involved):

Dear Mom, Dad, and Family:

Writing this letter is one of the most difficult things I have ever done. I love you all so very much and do not want to hurt you in any way, but there is something I must say. Mom and Dad, you have always taught me to tell the truth no matter what happens, so the time has come that I must be honest with all of you about who I really am.

These last several years have been the most difficult of my entire life. While you all know I am struggling with depression, the reason behind my depression has been my agonizing over whether or not I am gay. I have prayed, fasted, studied the scriptures, spent many hours reading books and magazines and talking to many of my friends, trying to find answers to my questions. I have come to the conclusion that I am gay and have always been so. Even though I haven't wanted to admit that I'm homosexual, because I thought it was a sin to be repented of, I've recently realized that being gay is who I really am. I have learned that my homosexuality is just like someone else being heterosexual. It is something that we have no con-trol over—it is a part of who we are. In the very same way I have blond hair and freckles and am six feet tall, I am also gay. I believe it is the way God intended me to be.

I'm not sure where we go from here, but I love each of you, and I also want you to know that I still love the Church as well. I have a testimony and believe that in time the Church will come to understand that their stand against homosexuality is outdated—just like they did with the blacks receiving the priesthood. Please don't hate me and please don't try to change me. I have tried going to counseling and have spoken to my bishops over the last several years, but it hasn't helped. Trying to help me not be gay is like asking a man who is attracted to his wife to direct his affections towards another man—it doesn't work. I'm really the same person I have always been, just more honest with myself and now with you.

I know this will be hard for everyone and I totally understand, but I know it is the best thing for everyone concerned. Please don't hate me. I want so much to be a part of the family and to love and be loved by you.[2]

My heart goes out to this young man and to his family and friends as well. He believes he is homosexual and has found some seasonal peace in being "honest" about who he believes himself to be. The real tragedy of this story, as well as the doctrinal reality in it, is that this young man has been deceived into being *honest about a lie.* He has come to believe and act upon the false notion that being homosexual is the way God intended him to be and that change is not necessary or even possible. Although this young man may have a biological predisposition for some of the physical and emotional characteristics that sometimes accompany the homosexual lifestyle, it is both a doctrinal truth and a scientific fact that his biology does not force him to engage in homosexual relationships. This young man may indeed be more susceptible to homosexual temptation than many other young men his age, and he may not have capriciously chosen to think and to feel the way he does, but the doctrinal fact is that he is "free to act for [himself]—*to choose* the way of everlasting death or the way of eternal life" (2 Nephi 10:23; emphasis added).

Elder Dallin H. Oaks has taught:

> Different persons have different physical characteristics and different susceptibilities to the various physical and emotional pressures we may encounter in our childhood and adult environments. We did not choose these personal susceptibilities either, but we do choose and will be accountable for the attitudes, priorities, behavior, and "lifestyle" we engraft upon them.[3]

The Lord and His prophets have taught that God did not create His children to be gay or lesbian and that for those who suffer with this affliction, change is possible. Also, contrary to what the young man in the story found in his own research, reliable scientific research supports the doctrinal truth that change is possible—someone who experiences same-sex attraction can work towards, and in time experience, a change in sexual orientation.

In 1973 Dr. Robert Spitzer was a leader in the mental health community who led the effort to have homosexuality removed from the American Psychiatric Association's official diagnostic manual of mental disorders. At that time Dr. Spitzer, a psychiatrist by training, believed that homosexuality was not something that could or should be corrected but was to be accepted and acknowledged.

Some thirty years later, Dr. Spitzer, by then professor of psychiatry and chief of biometrics at Columbia University in New York City, changed his opinion. He based his conclusion on his work with two hundred men and women who experienced a significant change in sexual orientation and who maintained the change for more than five years. Dr. Spitzer stated: "Like most psychiatrists I thought homosexual behavior could be resisted—but that no one could really change their sexual orientation. I now believe that's untrue—some people can and do change."[4] His conclusions are supported by many similar studies and reviews, including research conducted by a Latter-day Saint clinical professor in the department of psychiatry at the University of Utah, Dr. A. Dean Byrd.[5]

"Change is possible," as an official Church publication points out,[6] but it is often a long and difficult process. As with all our challenges in morality, the Lord stands ready to comfort us, give us strength, and offer counsel. The Savior has said: "Yea, verily, I say unto you, if ye will come unto me ye shall have eternal life. Behold, mine arm of mercy is extended towards you, and whosoever will come, him will I receive; and blessed are those who come unto me" (3 Nephi 9:14).

BORN THAT WAY OR BORN AGAIN?

Some time ago I had the privilege of counseling with a man who had struggled with homosexual thoughts and feelings for most of his life. On several occasions he had also acted on his feelings and become sexually involved with other men. This man, like most people I have worked with who struggle with same-sex attraction, had been taught that he had been "born that way," but he struggled to reconcile this prevalent belief with the teachings of the scriptures, his Church leaders, and the love of a remarkable wife. I worked with him for the better part of two years and then moved out of state, but we continued to stay in contact.

Through the time I counseled with him and the years that followed, he experienced a roller-coaster of success and failure. Eventually he got to a place in his life where he had refrained from sexual involvement with another man for an entire year. Not only had he stopped having immoral physical relationships but he had also experienced a remarkable decrease in homosexual thoughts and feelings as well.

During one of our conversations about how he had been able to achieve such remarkable success in overcoming his sexual attraction to other men, I asked him whether he believed he had been "born that way." His answer was more than I expected. "Dan," he said, "I'm not sure whether I was born homosexual or not, but what I do know is that I feel I have been *born again*." This man had discovered what fellow Church member Erin Eldridge had discovered in her battle to overcome same-sex attraction:

> Once considered a "homosexual," I have changed in many ways. I, like the people of King Benjamin, believe the words that have been spoken by the prophets and

"know of their surety and truth, because of the Spirit of the Lord Omnipotent, which has wrought a mighty change in [me], or in [my heart], that [I] have no more disposition to do evil, but to do good continually." I am "willing to enter into a covenant with [my] God to do his will, and to be obedient to his commandments in all things that he shall command [me], all the remainder of [my] days." For I "say that [my heart has been] changed through faith on his name; therefore, [I am] born of him and have become his [daughter]." (Mosiah 5:2, 5, 7.)[7]

My friend admitted that there were times when he still felt what he called the "tug" to indulge in homosexual thoughts, feelings, and actions, but as long as he kept himself connected to God through living the gospel of Christ, he was able to resist the temptation. He also found that as he continued to draw upon God's power to resist temptation and not rely solely on his own strength or on the strength of those who were trying to help him, the temptation lessened.

His insight into overcoming temptation illustrates the contrast between the Book of Mormon and the New Testament with respect to temptation. Carefully read the following two verses and notice the significant doctrinal difference between them:

There hath no temptation taken you but such as is common to man: but God is faithful, who will not suffer you to be tempted above that ye are able; but will with the temptation also make a way to escape, that ye may be able to bear it. (1 Corinthians 10:13)

But that ye would humble yourselves before the Lord, and call on his holy name, and watch and pray continually, that ye may not be tempted above that which ye can bear, and thus be led by the Holy Spirit, becoming humble, meek, submissive, patient, full of love and all long-suffering. (Alma 13:28)

What the apostle Paul taught is true. God does "make a way to escape" and He will not allow us to be tempted with more than we are able to bear, but we must understand that these promises are *conditional* upon our watching and praying continually and following the direction of the Spirit and those who lead us. Most of us eventually realize that if we don't do our part to stay connected to God, we are much more likely to give in to one temptation or another.

The word *religion* is a combination of the words *re* ("again") and *ligare* ("connect"), thus meaning to "reconnect" or to "tie back."[8] Just as a ligament (also from *ligare*) connects one bone to another, so our *religion* is ultimately about our relationship (being connected) to God and our reliance upon Him for strength to overcome temptation.

Another great truth I have learned from working with those who struggle with same-sex attraction is that even though we may be doing the very best we can to live the gospel and striving diligently to overcome the various sins and weaknesses with which we all wrestle, progress is often slow and sometimes even imperceptible. President Ezra Taft Benson once stated:

We must be careful, as we seek to become more and more godlike, that we do not become discouraged and lose hope. *Becoming Christlike is a lifetime pursuit and very often involves growth and change that is slow, almost imperceptible.* The scriptures record remarkable accounts of men whose lives changed dramatically, in an instant, as it were: Alma the Younger, Paul on the road to Damascus, Enos praying far into the night, King Lamoni. Such astonishing examples of the power to change even those steeped in sin give confidence that the Atonement can reach even those deepest in despair.

But we must be cautious as we discuss these remarkable examples. Though they are real and powerful, they are the exception more than the rule. For every Paul, for every Enos, and for every King Lamoni, there are hundreds and thousands of people who find the process of repentance much more subtle, much more imperceptible. Day by day they move closer to the Lord, little realizing they are building a godlike life. . . . They are like the Lamanites, who the Lord said "were baptized with fire and with the Holy Ghost, and they knew it not." (3 Ne. 9:20; italics added.)[9]

It is doctrinally possible that such problems as same-sex attraction and other weaknesses and addictions with which we struggle could be taken from us in an instant, but most often change is a gradual process that may not be complete until after the resurrection. The Prophet Joseph Smith taught:

> When you climb a ladder, you must begin at the bottom, and ascend step by step until you arrive at the top; and so it is with the principles of the Gospel: you must begin with the first, and go on until you learn all the principles of exaltation. But it will be a great while after you have passed through the vail [sic] before you will have learned them. It is not all to be comprehended in this world: it will be a great work to learn our salvation and exaltation even beyond the grave.[10]

Some struggle with same-sex attraction to the degree that they have chosen not to actively pursue heterosexual relationships and choose instead to remain celibate, believing that they may not be completely whole until after the resurrection (Matthew 19:12). President Gordon B. Hinckley has wisely stated, "Marriage should not be viewed as a therapeutic step to solve problems such as homosexual inclinations or practices, which first should clearly be overcome with a firm and fixed determination never to slip to such practices again."[11]

It is important to understand that how and when the Lord chooses to bless us is His choice. The Lord counseled the Prophet Joseph Smith:

> Therefore, sanctify yourselves that your minds become single to God, and the days will come that you shall see him; for he will unveil his face unto you, and it

shall be *in his own time, and in his own way, and according
to his own will.* (D&C 88:68; emphasis added)

The apostle Paul recorded that he had asked the Lord to
remove his unidentified "thorn in the flesh" three different
times without success, only to learn that the Lord had a divine
design in allowing his struggle to continue:

> And lest I should be exalted above measure through
> the abundance of the revelations, there was given to me
> a thorn in the flesh, the messenger of Satan to buffet me,
> lest I should be exalted above measure.
>
> For this thing I besought the Lord thrice, that it
> might depart from me.
>
> And he said unto me, My grace is sufficient for thee:
> for my strength is made perfect in weakness. Most gladly
> therefore will I rather glory in my infirmities, that the
> power of Christ may rest upon me.
>
> Therefore I take pleasure in infirmities, in reproaches,
> in necessities, in persecutions, in distresses for Christ's
> sake: for when I am weak, then am I strong. (2 Corinthi-
> ans 12:7–10)

HOMOSEXUALITY DEFINED

Many years ago a young man cautiously and tearfully
shared with me the sad reality that when he was ten years old
he had been sexually molested by an older man. In addition to
questions about whether his parents should know and if the

incident needed to be reported to the police, his main question was, "Does what happened to me mean that I'm gay?"

This sixteen-year-old young man had been living with the fear that because he had had sexual experience with another male, he was homosexual. It was my privilege to explain to him the liberating truth that although many men and women who describe themselves as "homosexual" were abused as children, sexual experience with someone of the same sex does not make one "homosexual." I also helped him understand that the term "homosexual" isn't a *noun* used to describe who a person is but is more appropriately used as an *adjective* to describe "erotic thoughts, feelings, and behavior directed toward persons of the same sex."[12]

Elder Dallin H. Oaks explained:

> We should note that the words *homosexual, lesbian,* and *gay* are adjectives to describe particular thoughts, feelings, or behaviors. We should refrain from using these words as nouns to identify particular conditions or specific persons. Our religious doctrine dictates this usage. It is wrong to use these words to denote a *condition,* because this implies that a person is consigned by birth to a circumstance in which he or she has no choice in respect to the critically important matter of sexual *behavior.*[13]

By way of definition, it may also be helpful to note that *homosexual* usually refers to the sexual behavior of males with males and females with females. The word *gay* generally, but not always, refers to male homosexual behavior, and *lesbian* refers to the homosexual behavior of females. Although the word *homosexual* is not found in scripture, the terms "effeminate" and "abusers of themselves with mankind" in the following passage of scripture are generally understood to describe the different roles assumed in a homosexual relationship:

> Know ye not that the unrighteous shall not inherit the kingdom of God? Be not deceived: neither fornicators, nor idolaters, nor adulterers, nor *effeminate,* nor *abusers of themselves with mankind,*
>
> Nor thieves, nor covetous, nor drunkards, nor revilers, nor extortioners, shall inherit the kingdom of God. (1 Corinthians 6:9–10; emphasis added)

Other scriptural references concerning the practice of homosexuality include Genesis 19:1–29; Leviticus 18:22; Leviticus 20:13; 1 Corinthians 6:9; and 1 Timothy 1:10. Perhaps the most detailed and complete scriptural commentary on same-sex attraction is in the apostle Paul's epistle to the Romans. Paul warned those who "[suppress] the truth in unrighteousness" (Romans 1:18) and continued by describing the error of both gay and lesbian behavior:

> Professing themselves to be wise, they became fools. . . .
>
> Wherefore God also gave them up to uncleanness through the lusts of their own hearts, to dishonour their own bodies between themselves:
>
> Who changed the truth of God into a lie, and

worshipped and served the creature more than the Creator, who is blessed for ever. . . .

For this cause God gave them up unto vile affections: for even their women did change the natural use into that which is against nature:

And likewise also the men, leaving the natural use of the woman, burned in their lust one toward another; men with men working that which is unseemly, and receiving in themselves that recompence of their error which was meet. (Romans 1:22, 24–27)

Latter-day prophets and apostles have also spoken concerning the evils of sexual immorality by clearly teaching that any kind of sexual relations outside of marriage, whether such relations be homosexual or heterosexual, is sinful. Though they are less serious, immoral thoughts and feelings need to be overcome as well:

> The Lord's law of moral conduct is abstinence outside of lawful marriage and fidelity within marriage. Sexual relations are proper only between husband and wife appropriately expressed within the bonds of marriage. Any other sexual contact, including fornication, adultery, and homosexual and lesbian behavior, is sinful. Those who persist in such practices or who influence others to do so are subject to Church discipline.
>
> We remind you of scriptures that make clear the relationship between one's thoughts and actions (see Matthew 15:19; Mosiah 4:29–30; Alma 12:14; 3 Nephi

12:28; D&C 121:45). There is a distinction between immoral thoughts and feelings and participating in either immoral heterosexual or any homosexual behavior. However, such thoughts and feelings, regardless of their causes, can and should be overcome and sinful behavior should be eliminated.[14]

This statement of the First Presidency indicates that immoral thoughts and feelings may be somewhat less serious than immoral behavior, yet they are closely connected and need to be dealt with appropriately. King Benjamin warned:

> But this much I can tell you, that if ye do not watch yourselves, and your thoughts, and your words, and your deeds, and observe the commandments of God, and continue in the faith of what ye have heard concerning the coming of our Lord, even unto the end of your lives, ye must perish. And now, O man, remember, and perish not. (Mosiah 4:30)

HOW SHOULD WE RESPOND?

The best response to any crisis begins years before it actually confronts us. I am often reminded of the following counsel from the Lord as I work with individuals, married couples, and families in crisis:

> They were slow to hearken unto the voice of the Lord their God; therefore, the Lord their God is slow to hearken unto their prayers, to answer them in the day of

their trouble. In the day of their peace they esteemed lightly my counsel; but, in the day of their trouble, of necessity they feel after me. (D&C 101:7–8)

The best time to prepare for a heart attack is years before it occurs, not the minute chest pains begin.

The First Presidency has stated:

> Parents should teach their children the sacred nature of procreative powers and instill in them a desire to be chaste in thought and deed. A correct understanding of the divinely appointed roles of men and women will fortify all against sinful practices. Our only real safety, physically and spiritually, lies in keeping the Lord's commandments.[15]

THE GREAT PLAN OF THE ETERNAL GOD

The Book of Mormon prophet Alma taught: "God gave unto them commandments, *after* having made known unto them the plan of redemption" (Alma 12:32; emphasis added). The teachings and commandments God has given pertaining to sexuality (and any other topic, for that matter) will have much more meaning if we have a broader understanding of why He has given them and how they fit into the larger picture of eternity. Speaking to a gathering of educators in the Church Educational System, Elder Boyd K. Packer stated:

> Why are we commanded *to do* some things, and why are we commanded *not* to do other things? A knowledge

of the plan of happiness, even in outline form, can give young minds a "why."

A parent once angrily scolded a child for a serious mistake, saying, "Why on earth did you do such a thing?" The child answered, "If I'd had a 'why,' I wouldn't have done it."

Providing your students [or others] with a collection of unrelated truths will hurt as much as it helps. Provide a basic feeling for the whole plan [of salvation], even with just a few details, and it will help them ever so much more. Let them know what it's all about; then they will have the "why."

Most of the difficult questions we face in the Church right now, and we could list them . . . cannot be answered without some knowledge of the plan as a background.[16]

When many of us think of the plan of salvation, we remember lessons accompanied by blackboard diagrams of several circles connected by various lines illustrating our progression from premortal life to celestial glory. As helpful as these illustrations are, if not used wisely and understood correctly, they could distract us from understanding the depth as well as the breadth of the Lord's profound plan. Elder Neal A. Maxwell has observed:

Conversationally, we reference this great design almost too casually at times; we even sketch its rude outlines on chalkboards and paper as if it were the floor plan for an addition to one's house. However, when we really take time to ponder the Plan, it is breathtaking and over-powering! Indeed, I, for one, cannot decide which creates in me the most awe—its very vastness or its intricate, individualized detail.[17]

Both ancient and modern prophets have taught that "the great plan of the eternal God" (Alma 34:9) is based on the doctrines of the Creation, the Fall, and the Atonement. Elder Bruce R. McConkie described these three doctrines as "the three pillars of eternity" and stated that they "are inseparably woven together into one grand tapestry known as the eternal plan of salvation" (Alma 18:36–39; 22:12–14).[18] Understanding what the prophet Nephi called "the great and eternal plan of deliverance" (2 Nephi 11:5) can serve as a helpful foundation for any discussion of same-sex attraction.

THE DOCTRINE OF CREATION

We are sons and daughters of a Heavenly Father and Mother who created us "male and female" (D&C 20:18; Moses 2:27; Genesis 1:27). Thus, "gender is an essential characteristic of individual premortal, mortal, and eternal identity and purpose."[19] President Harold B. Lee affirmed that "the Lord created male and female, and He didn't have a woman's soul trapped in a man's body, or vice versa."[20] But even though we understand that we were male and female before we were born and that gender is not simply a social or physiological phenomenon, the cultural definitions of what it means to be a "man" or a "woman" have become a part of the gender confusion that is related to problems of same-sex attraction. To illustrate this problem, consider the following two lists:

LIST 1	LIST 2
Affectionate	Strong
Compassionate	Decisive
Gentle	Confidant
Sensitive	Controlled
Tender	Independent
Warm	Courageous
Understanding	Consistent

Many individuals, when asked which of the two lists is more descriptive of a "female" personality, will choose the first, and when asked which list is more representative of a "male" personality, will choose the second. Because the prophets have clearly taught that men and women were purposely created with gender-related differences, perhaps a more important question is, "Which list of characteristics best describes the Savior?" Of course, the answer is that Jesus Christ is the perfect embodiment of all that is good on any list, and it is our privilege and responsibility to do all that we can to become like Him.

So much of what the world teaches that a man or woman should be is a counterfeit of what the Lord and His servants have taught. Even though the following counsel from the prophet Alma contains characteristics that might be considered more "feminine" by some, the Lord would have both men and women follow the counsel contained therein:

And now I would that ye should be *humble,* and be *submissive* and *gentle; easy to be entreated; full of patience* and *long-suffering;* being *temperate* in all things; being *diligent* in keeping the commandments of God at all times; asking for whatsoever things ye stand in need, both spiritual and temporal; always returning thanks unto God for whatsoever things ye do receive. (Alma 7:23; emphasis added)

A young man should never be belittled for being gentle but helped and encouraged to also be strong. A young woman should never be ridiculed for being strong but helped and encouraged to also be gentle. The Prophet Joseph Smith taught, "If men do not comprehend the character of God, they do not comprehend themselves."[21] Jesus Christ was and is both strong and gentle, and He would have us be even as He is. "What manner of men ought ye to be?" the Savior asks. "Verily I say unto you, even as I am" (3 Nephi 27:27).

THE DOCTRINE OF THE FALL

The Latter-day Saint doctrine of the fall of Adam and Eve has some significant differences from the same doctrine taught by others. The central difference is that latter-day scripture and the words of our modern prophets clearly state that the Fall was both necessary and essential to the Lord's plan. The prophet Lehi taught:

And now, behold, if Adam had not transgressed he would not have fallen, but he would have remained in the garden of Eden. And all things which were created must have remained in the same state in which they were after they were created; and they must have remained forever, and had no end.

And they would have had no children; wherefore they would have remained in a state of innocence, having no joy, for they knew no misery; doing no good, for they knew no sin. But behold, all things have been done in the wisdom of him who knoweth all things.

Adam fell that men might be; and men are, that they might have joy. (2 Nephi 2:22–25)

Many faiths espouse the idea that if Adam and Eve had not partaken of the fruit of the tree of knowledge of good and evil, they and their posterity (including you and me) would still be living blissfully in the Garden of Eden. Lehi, however, tells us that without the Fall we would have never been born into mortality. He continues his discourse by explaining the necessity of opposites, that righteousness can be understood only in relation to wickedness, happiness in opposition to misery, good in relation to bad, and so forth. "Wherefore," Lehi states, "all things must needs be a compound in one" (2 Nephi 2:11).

President Spencer W. Kimball further explained the necessity of opposition:

> Is there not wisdom in his giving us trials that we might rise above them, responsibilities that we might achieve, work to harden our muscles, sorrows to try our souls? Are we not exposed to temptations to test our

strength, sickness that we might learn patience, death that we might be immortalized and glorified?[22]

The Lord allows temptation to exist as a part of the test of mortality. Through the prophet Brigham Young the Lord taught the early Saints: "My people must be tried in *all things,* that they may be prepared to receive the glory that I have for them, even the glory of Zion; and he that will not bear chastisement is not worthy of my kingdom" (D&C 136:31; emphasis added).

Just as Devil's Gate marked a difficult place on the pioneer trail in 1847, so same-sex attraction may be the challenge some Saints face in the present. For others, the challenge may be a stronger than normal attraction to members of the opposite sex or a predisposition for alcohol or other drugs. For still others, trials may have to do with depression, anxiety, or an insatiable desire for wealth, power, position, or intellectual prowess. As the apostle Paul taught, "Temptation . . . is common to man" (1 Corinthians 10:13). We all have temptation—we are just tempted in different ways.

Speaking of the choices made by Adam and Eve to partake of the fruit of the tree of knowledge of good and evil while in the Garden of Eden, the prophet Lehi explained:

> And to bring about his eternal purposes in the end of man, after he had created our first parents, and the beasts of the field and the fowls of the air, and in fine, all things which are created, it must needs be that there was an

opposition; even the forbidden fruit in opposition to the tree of life; the one being sweet and the other bitter.

Wherefore, the Lord God gave unto man that he should act for himself. Wherefore, man could not act for himself save it should be that he was enticed by the one or the other. (2 Nephi 2:15–16)

From the Pearl of Great Price we learn that the Lord instructed Adam that inasmuch as his posterity would be conceived into a world of sin, they would be allowed to "taste the bitter, that they may know to prize the good" (Moses 6:55). And because we too have the choice between good and evil and "all have sinned, and come short of the glory of God" (Romans 3:23), each of us is in vital need of a Savior.

THE DOCTRINE OF THE ATONEMENT OF CHRIST

Erin Eldridge, author of the perceptive book *Born That Way?* stated that her deliverance from same-sex attraction was more than simply a change of her behavior. It was a change of her heart, made possible through the atonement of Jesus Christ:

> Yes, even those who have been considered "homosexual" can change. And I, for one, will never go back. I can say with Alma, "After wading through much tribulation, repenting nigh unto death, the Lord in mercy hath seen fit to snatch me out of an everlasting burning, and I am born of God. My soul hath been redeemed from the gall of bitterness and bonds of iniquity. I was in the darkest

abyss; but now I behold the marvelous light of God. My soul was racked with eternal torment; but I am snatched, and my soul is pained no more" (Mosiah 27:28–29).[23]

After describing the various sins that would characterize those who would be denied entrance into "the kingdom of God," including the "effeminate" and the "abusers of themselves with mankind," the apostle Paul stated: "*And such were some of you,* but ye are washed, but ye are sanctified, but ye are justified in the name of the Lord Jesus, and by the Spirit of our God" (1 Corinthians 6:11; emphasis added). Paul's words bear testimony that among the Corinthian Saints were some who had overcome homosexuality through the atoning sacrifice of Jesus Christ. A modern-day apostle, Elder Richard G. Scott, testified that through Christ change continues to be possible in our day:

> I cannot comprehend his power, his majesty, his perfections. But I do understand something of his love, his compassion, his mercy. There is no burden he cannot lift. There is no heart he cannot purify and fill with joy. There is no life he cannot cleanse and restore when one is obedient to his teachings.[24]

Not only is change possible but President Boyd K. Packer assured us that it is also possible to repent and receive forgiveness of our sins: "Save for the exception of the very few who defect to perdition, there is no habit, no addiction, no rebellion, no transgression, no apostasy, no crime, exempted from the promise of complete forgiveness."[25]

Formal Church discipline may be necessary for those who are involved in homosexual relationships, but it is important to remember that the intent of such action is redemptive, not punitive. The intention is to bless, not to belittle or berate. Justice is as much an expression of a loving God (and a loving Church leader) as is mercy. Probation, disfellowshipment, or even excommunication can be a part of the healing process.

DELIVERED FROM BONDAGE

In my ecclesiastical duties of working with individuals and families who face a wide variety of challenges (including same-sex attraction), I have found the account of the deliverance of Alma and his people from bondage to be very helpful. After the people had been in captivity for some time, "the voice of the Lord came to them in their afflictions, saying: Lift up your heads and be of good comfort, for I know of the covenant which ye have made unto me; and I will *covenant* with my people and deliver them out of bondage" (Mosiah 24:13; emphasis added).

From this verse we read that the first key to deliverance for Alma's people, and for each of us, is to be in *a covenant relationship* with God. Earlier in the Book of Mosiah we read that the covenant Alma and his people had entered into included a promise to "serve him and keep his commandments" (Mosiah 18:10), evidenced by their desire to "come into the fold of

God, and to be called his people" and a willingness to "bear one another's burdens, that they may be light" (Mosiah 18:8).

We also read that this covenant included a "willing[ness] to mourn with those that mourn; yea, and [to] comfort those that stand in need of comfort, and to stand as witnesses of God at all times and in all things, and in all places that ye may be in, even until death" (Mosiah 18:9). In return the Lord promised Alma and his people that they would be "redeemed of God, and be numbered with those of the first resurrection, [and] have eternal life" (Mosiah 18:9). The Lord promised them, and this is key, that He would "pour out his Spirit more abundantly upon [them]" (Mosiah 18:10).

Early in my career as a therapist and as a young bishop, I was much more likely to provide specific counsel to those I was working with than I am now. Though there are several basic principles, policies, and practices I attempt to help individuals understand, my main objective is to help them fully accept the Savior and to learn to live in such a way that they may have the Holy Ghost to guide them. The prophet Nephi taught, "If ye will enter in by the way, and receive the Holy Ghost, it will show unto you all things what ye should do" (2 Nephi 32:5).

No matter how we are serving those who are struggling—whether as Church leader, family member, therapist, or friend—we need to be sure that we too are striving to be directed by the Holy Ghost. The prophet Alma, reflecting on his early days when he had been deceived by wicked King Noah and become one of his priests, stated, "And also trust no one to be your teacher nor your minister, except he be a man of

God, walking in his ways and keeping his commandments" (Mosiah 23:14). Alma's words underscore the importance of working with priesthood leaders, trusted professionals, and friends who can be relied upon to offer counsel and support consistent with the teachings of the Savior.

Alma and his followers were not delivered from their burdens immediately, but they were endowed with an increase in strength to bear them. The Lord said to them, "I will also ease the burdens which are put upon your shoulders, that even you cannot feel them upon your backs, even while you are in bondage; and this will I do that ye may stand as witnesses for me hereafter, and that ye may know of a surety that I, the Lord God, do visit my people in their afflictions" (Mosiah 24:14). As Alma's people enjoyed the fruits of the Spirit and were able to "submit cheerfully and with patience to all the will of the Lord" (Mosiah 24:15), they were eventually delivered from bondage to the Lamanites and were returned to their families from whom they had been lost for a generation (Mosiah 24:25).

The most significant insight from this text that has been helpful in my own life and as I have attempted to help others is in Mosiah 24:21: "Yea, and in the valley of Alma they poured out their thanks to God because he had been merciful unto them, and eased their burdens, and had delivered them out of bondage; for they were in bondage, and *none could deliver them except it were the Lord their God*" (emphasis added). Alma and his people had not yet arrived in Zarahemlah, but they had been delivered. They were still on their journey, as all of us are, but they knew in whom they could trust, the only Person who had and could deliver them: the Lord Jesus Christ.

CONCLUSION

There are some questions associated with same-sex attraction for which we do not have answers, but there are many things we do know. Elder Neal A. Maxwell taught that although a multitude of factors influence what we think, how we feel, and what we do, there will always be a part of us that remains free:

> Of course our genes, circumstances, and environments matter very much, and they shape us significantly. Yet there remains an inner zone in which we are sovereign, unless we abdicate. In this zone lies the essence of our individuality and our personal accountability.[26]

Discovering the answers to the questions associated with the issue of same-sex attraction will require our best efforts, most compassionate responses, and faithful reliance on the Lord and the counsel of His servants.

CHAPTER SIX

Can a Person Who Has Been Abused Be Healed?

In what may have been one of the first public discourses of the
Savior's mortal ministry, He stood before the people of
Nazareth and read from the writings of the prophet Isaiah:
"The Spirit of the Lord is upon me, because he hath anointed
me to preach the gospel to the poor; he hath sent me to heal
the brokenhearted, to preach deliverance to the captives, and
recovering of sight to the blind, to set at liberty them that are
bruised" (Luke 4:18; see also Isaiah 61:1–2). The Gospel of
Luke records that Jesus then stated, "This day is this scripture
fulfilled in your ears" (Luke 4:21). By first reading Isaiah's
prophecy and then making this statement, Jesus formally identified Himself to His family, friends, neighbors, and to the
world as the Christ, the long-awaited Messiah.

Partly because Jesus had spent much of His childhood
among the residents of Nazareth and they knew Him simply
as the son of Mary and Joseph, they rejected Him as the Christ
and attempted to take His life. Luke states, "All they in the

synagogue, when they heard these things, were filled with wrath and rose up, and thrust him out of the city, and led him unto the brow of the hill . . . that they might cast him down headlong" (Luke 4:28–29).

The account of Jesus' escape is particularly important for our study of abuse, for not only is it the mortal Messiah's first formal declaration of His divine anointing but it is also the first recorded incidence of people attempting to abuse Him and to take His life. The abuse Jesus would yet receive in the years that followed culminated in His being betrayed, mocked, spat upon, scourged, and crucified.

Isaiah's prophecies of the coming Messiah referred to His divine ability to "bind up the brokenhearted. . . . to comfort all that mourn," and "to give unto them beauty for ashes" (Isaiah 61:1–3) as they also described the sorrow and rejection the Savior would experience as a mortal man:

> He is despised and rejected of men; a man of sorrows, and acquainted with grief: and we [the Jews] hid as it were our faces from him; he was despised, and we esteemed him not.
>
> Surely he hath borne our griefs, and carried our sorrows: yet we did esteem him stricken, smitten of God, and afflicted. (Isaiah 53:3–4)

From these few scriptural accounts, and many others as well, it is clear that Jesus Christ was intimately familiar with abuse. In addition to suffering for our sins (1 Peter 3:18), He is "the hope of Israel, the saviour thereof in time of trouble"

(Jeremiah 14:8). He thus has the understanding, ability, and power to heal those who have been abused.

In addition to examples from the life and teachings of Jesus relative to the experience of abuse, as well as other scriptural counsel, our latter-day prophets and other leaders have spoken on this sobering topic. We learn that in very deed those who have been abused and those who are attempting to help them may understand and experience "the work of miracles and of healing" (Mormon 1:13) made possible through the gospel of Jesus Christ.

JESUS CHRIST COMPREHENDS ALL SIN, SORROW, AND SUFFERING

We understand that Jesus gave His life freely (John 10:18) and that His death was a necessary part of the Lord's plan for our redemption (John 3:14–16). President John Taylor helps us understand why the Savior allowed Himself to be abused and to suffer as He did:

> I will take him [Jesus] for an example, and ask why he was persecuted and afflicted? Why was he put to death? We are told by the apostle that it was necessary for him, of whom are all things, to make the captain of our salvation perfect through suffering. It was absolutely necessary that he should pass through this state, and be subject to all the weaknesses of the flesh,—that he should also be subjected to the buffetings of Satan the same as we are, and pass through all the trials incident to humanity,

and thereby comprehend the weakness and the true character of human nature, with all its faults and foibles, that we might have a faithful High Priest that would know how to deliver those that are tempted; and hence one of the apostles, in speaking of him, says, "For we have not a High Priest which cannot be touched with the feelings of our infirmities, but was in all points tempted like as we are, yet without sin." (Hebrews 4:15.)[1]

The prophet Alma taught a similar doctrine:

And he [Jesus Christ] shall go forth, suffering pains and afflictions and temptations of every kind; and this that the word might be fulfilled which saith he will take upon him the pains and the sicknesses of his people.

And he will take upon him death, that he may loose the bands of death which bind his people; and he will take upon him their infirmities, that his bowels may be filled with mercy, according to the flesh, that he may know according to the flesh how to succor his people according to their infirmities. (Alma 7:11–12)

Jesus suffered in every way—physically, emotionally, and spiritually—and because of His sufferings, our Savior is intimately and infinitely prepared to bless and to heal those who suffer in similar ways. Not only can the Savior identify with the pain we feel because of His similar experience but *He has felt the very pain that we feel* and stands ready to bless us. After acknowledging the trials and tribulations the Prophet Joseph had experienced and would yet experience, Jesus taught the Prophet that He, Jesus, had "descended below them all" (D&C 122:8). Elder Merrill J. Bateman has said, "In the garden and on the cross, Jesus saw each of us and not only bore our sins, but also experienced our deepest feelings so that he would know how to comfort and strengthen us."[2] "Consequently," Elder Bateman also said, "if one of us has a special problem, it is not possible for him or her to say, 'no one knows what I am experiencing. No one understands my pain and suffering.' The Lord knows! He not only knows the depth of your experience, He knows how to succor you because of his suffering."[3] Our Savior "descended below all things, in that he comprehended all things, that he might be in all and through all things, the light of truth" (D&C 88:6).

ABUSE DEFINED

"Abuse in any form is tragic and in opposition to the teachings of the Savior. Abuse is the physical, emotional, sexual, or spiritual mistreatment of others. It may not only harm the body, but it can deeply affect the mind and spirit, destroying faith and causing confusion, doubt, mistrust, guilt, and fear."[4] This definition, provided in a special publication commissioned and approved by the First Presidency, shows that abuse is much more than the physical violence we often associate with such behavior; abuse can also be emotional, sexual, and/or spiritual. The following familiar definition of abuse from the Doctrine and Covenants is directed to priesthood holders, but it is a meaningful warning against all forms of abuse:

The rights of the priesthood are inseparably connected with the powers of heaven, and that the powers of
heaven cannot be controlled nor handled only upon the
principles of righteousness.

That they may be conferred upon us, it is true; but
*when we undertake to cover our sins, or to gratify our pride,
our vain ambition, or to exercise control or dominion or
compulsion upon the souls of the children of men, in any
degree of unrighteousness,* behold, the heavens withdraw
themselves; the Spirit of the Lord is grieved; and when it
is withdrawn, Amen to the priesthood or the authority of
that man. (D&C 121:36–37; emphasis added)

When most of us hear the word *abuse* we think of the mistreatment of children, but abuse can also be experienced by
others as well, such as spouses, siblings, neighbors, co-workers,
and the elderly. President Gordon B. Hinckley spoke strongly
concerning the abuse of children:

I am satisfied that no other experiences of life draw
us nearer to heaven than those that exist between happy
parents and happy children.

My plea—and I wish I were more eloquent in voic-
ing it—is a plea to save the children. Too many of them
walk with pain and fear, in loneliness and despair.
Children need sunlight. They need happiness. They need
love and nurture. They need kindness and refreshment
and affection. Every home, regardless of the cost of the

house, can provide an environment of love which will be an environment of salvation.[5]

President Thomas S. Monson brought to the forefront two additional dimensions of this pernicious problem—the person who is guilty of perpetrating abuse, and individuals who know of the abuse but do not properly assist those involved:

> The Church does not condone such heinous and vile conduct. Rather, we condemn in the harshest of terms such treatment of God's precious children. Let the child be rescued, nurtured, loved, and healed. Let the offender be brought to justice, to accountability, for his actions and receive professional treatment to curtail such wicked and devilish conduct. When you and I know of such conduct and fail to take action to eradicate it, we become part of the problem. We share part of the guilt. We experience part of the punishment.[6]

THE ABUSER

The Savior spoke very clearly of those who abuse children: "But whoso shall offend one of these little ones which believe in me, it were better for him that a millstone were hanged about his neck, and that he were drowned in the depth of the sea" (Matthew 18:6). The Savior's strong words underscore the seriousness of the sin of abuse, for which there is no legitimate justifications. "Offend" in this passage has a broad meaning that includes actions and intentions beyond physical abuse. It can mean a physical assault of one kind or another, but it also can be interpreted as "to trip up," or "to cause to stumble." One Bible scholar has defined the word *offend* (*skandalizo* in Greek) in the following way: "to cause a person to begin to distrust and desert one whom he ought to trust and obey."[7] Such a definition echoes the words of the Book of Mormon prophet Jacob to an unrepentant group of Nephite husbands and fathers:

> Ye have broken the hearts of your tender wives, and *lost the confidence of your children,* because of your bad examples before them; and the sobbings of their hearts ascend up to God against you. And because of the strictness of the word of God, which cometh down against you, many hearts died, pierced with deep wounds. (Jacob 2:35; emphasis added)

SPIRITUAL ABUSE

In addition to the specters of physical, emotional, and sexual abuse, a most deceptive and destructive form of abuse is spiritual abuse. Whenever anyone attempts to use religious beliefs, practices, or authority as a means to "exercise control or dominion or compulsion upon the souls of the children of men, in any degree of unrighteousness" (D&C 121:37), he or she is guilty of spiritual abuse. Brother Carlfred Broderick, a faithful Latter-day Saint and a world-renowned marriage and family therapist, illustrates how easy it is for parents to spiritually abuse their children in the name of religion. On one occasion Dr. Broderick referred to a Jewish colleague for therapy an

LDS family who was having problems with a rebellious daughter. After encountering resistance from the parents to his counsel to "lighten up a little" with their rebellious teenager, the therapist sought Dr. Broderick's counsel:

> "Every time I suggest any movement in the direction
> of loosening up, they patiently explain to me that I just
> don't understand their religious obligation, as Mormon
> parents, to keep this kid in line. Frankly, I don't know
> how to deal with this. I don't want to attack their reli-
> gious beliefs, but the situation is explosive."[8]

Brother Broderick responded by suggesting the therapist express interest in teachings of the LDS Church, specifically, "the war in heaven." The therapist did so and called some time later, amazed at how well Brother Broderick's counsel had worked. The therapist indicated that even the rebellious teen had offered to share with him a copy of a book about the LDS faith with a picture of the family in the front. The therapist was most amazed with the mother's dramatic change. After describing how the mother had first shown great enthusiasm at the opportunity of sharing her beliefs about the "war in heaven," she experienced a sudden change. The therapist described what happened:

> "In seconds she had launched into some story about a
> council in heaven and two plans and she gets about three
> minutes into it and she stops cold in her tracks and gives
> me a funny look and says, 'All right, Doctor, you've made

your point.' From that moment on they were like putty in my hands. It was like magic. Carl, what is this war in heaven?"[9]

Obviously the mother had suddenly realized that what she was doing to control her daughter's behavior was similar to the strategy proposed by Satan in the premortal council and was a part of the adversary's plan to "destroy the agency of man" (Moses 4:3). Most of us have had similar experiences and can testify that the war in heaven is not over, and the battle for the souls of men continues in all families.

In addition to seeking to exert unrighteous *control,* spiritual abuse can also be the *neglect* of those whom we have the responsibility to bless. The prophet Jeremiah described leaders who abuse their people by neglecting their duty: "Woe be unto the pastors that destroy and scatter the sheep of my pasture! saith the Lord. . . . Ye have scattered my flock, and driven them away, and have not visited them. . . . And I will gather the remnant of my flock. . . . And I will set up shepherds over them which shall feed them: and they shall fear no more, nor be dismayed, neither shall they be lacking, saith the Lord" (Jeremiah 23:1–4).

Some priesthood and auxiliary leaders and teachers in the Church have been unable to gain the confidence, or have lost the trust, of their followers because of spiritually abusive behavior. Men and women have lost the love and confidence of their families because of "unrighteous dominion" (D&C 121:39). Ironically, these individuals may mistakenly believe they are being righteous spouses and parents, only to lose their families because of the very things they think they are doing to save them.

Generally, those who have been the recipients of unrighteous dominion have a difficult time following, respecting, or even learning from the individuals whom they perceive to have hurt them. This resentment sometimes spills over to other people who occupy similar positions, or to the organization of which the alleged abuser was a part. For example, if a father spiritually abuses his child in the name of the priesthood and the Church, the child may resist fully embracing the gospel and struggle with gaining or sustaining a testimony. As a ward and stake leader, I have sometimes had difficulty gaining the trust of individuals because of what they perceived as unrighteous dominion by their fathers, husbands, brothers, and previous priesthood leaders.

I may need to apologize to Zeniff one day, but every time I read his story in the Book of Mormon, I find myself wondering if what he describes as being "over-zealous to inherit the land of [his] fathers" (Mosiah 9:3; see also 7:1) contributed to the rebelliousness of his son, King Noah. Though it would be a denial of the doctrine of agency to place blame for all of Noah's problems on the overzealousness of his father, it is quite common for children who are the sons and daughters of spiritually abusive parents to rebel.

HUSBAND AND WIFE AS EQUAL PARTNERS

Instead of lovingly leading their families by "long-suffering, by gentleness and meekness, and by love unfeigned; by kindness, and pure knowledge . . . without hypocrisy, and without guile" (D&C 121:41–42), some abuse their families by leading in harsh and dictatorial ways. One common justification for this style of leadership in the home is based on a distortion of what it means to be the "head of the family." Such individuals often justify their abusive behavior by explaining that they are simply fulfilling their role as the head of the home in the same way a bishop leads a ward. These individuals mistakenly believe that the husband-wife relationship should mirror that of a bishop and his counselors. The wife may give her opinion, these individuals assert, but "the husband is the head of the wife" (Ephesians 5:23) and she should ultimately submit to him and to his decisions.

It is true that husbands and bishops are to preside in the home and in the Church, respectively, but equating the relationship of husband and wife to that of a bishop and his counselors is not the doctrine of the Church and can lead to serious problems. President Gordon B. Hinckley has said: "Marriage, in its truest sense, is a partnership of equals, with neither exercising dominion over the other, but, rather, with each encouraging and assisting the other in whatever responsibilities and aspirations he or she might have."[10]

Brother Carlfred Broderick described the instruction he received from Elder Boyd K. Packer to illustrate the principal difference between a man presiding at home and presiding in his Church responsibilities:

> Immediately after setting me apart as a stake president, Elder Boyd K. Packer sat me down to give me a few

points of advice on how to succeed in my new calling. I was fully prepared to be receptive to his counsel, but I couldn't help being taken aback by his first admonition.

"Now, President, I don't want you treating your wife like you do the stake."

I was mildly offended. I said, "I wasn't planning on treating either the stake or my wife badly."

"I know," he continued, "but you need to treat them well, differently. In the stake when a decision is to be made, you will seek the opinion of your counselors and other concerned individuals. Then you will prayerfully reach a decision on the matter, and they will all rally round and support you because you are the president and you have the mantle of authority. In your family when there is a decision to be made that affects everyone, you and your wife together will seek whatever counsel you might need, and together you will prayerfully come to a unified decision. If you ever pull priesthood rank on her you will have failed in your leadership."[11]

A husband and wife with whom I am acquainted could not agree on a name for their baby. The husband mistakenly thought it was his "priesthood privilege" to make the final decision and to give the baby the name he had chosen when he formally named and blessed the child during sacrament meeting. He was surprised when his bishop told him that he would not be able to perform the ordinance until he and his wife had mutually agreed on the name. After some time passed, this husband and wife finally agreed on a name, the ordinance was performed, and both the baby and the marriage were blessed. A husband isn't able to "pull rank" on his wife because he has no rank to pull.

A few years ago, in my calling as a stake president, I received approval from the First Presidency to extend a call to a wonderful man to serve as the bishop of one of our wards. When I issued the call to this man and his wife, he humbly asked if it would be permissible for his uncle to ordain him a bishop. I explained to him that the answer to that question depended upon what priesthood keys his uncle held. He reminded me that his uncle was someone of whom I was well aware—President Gordon B. Hinckley. I answered that having President Hinckley ordain him would be fine and that he was welcome to discuss the matter with his uncle, set the appropriate time, and proceed. I also told him that though I would like to be present for the ordination, my involvement wasn't really necessary and that the real issue should be President Hinckley's schedule and willingness to perform the ordination.

After discussing the matter with President Hinckley, the soon-to-be ordained bishop called me on the phone and reported that President Hinckley wanted to visit with me. I was surprised but happy to contact our beloved prophet. During the phone conversation, President Hinckley asked for my authorization to allow him to ordain his nephew to the office of bishop. I said something profound like, "President, you don't need my permission—please proceed in any manner you wish." President Hinckley gently corrected me and explained that his going ahead without my authorization was not the way priesthood keys were to be used.

I learned a lesson then that I will never forget. President Hinckley taught me that priesthood authority does not provide any license for unrighteous dominion of any kind, even when it is invited. President Hinckley, prophet, seer, revelator, and president of The Church of Jesus Christ of Latter-day Saints followed the Lord's prescribed program and was careful to exercise his sacred keys in the appropriate manner.

Whether it be the prophet of the Lord working with a stake president, a husband interacting with his wife, a parent rearing a child, or a Sunday School teacher teaching her class, there is a sacred order based on the love of God and neighbor and not the prideful love of self. Though it is true that the keys held by priesthood leaders give them the authority to direct someone of lesser authority, the same is not true in the relationship between husband and wife. The phrase "the husband is the head of the wife" is only a fraction of the sentence the apostle Paul wrote to the Saints at Ephesus. The complete statement reads, "For the husband is the head of the wife, even as Christ is the head of the church: and he is the saviour of the body" (Ephesians 5:23). For a husband and father to be the head of the wife and the family in the way that Christ is the head of the Church, the husband sacrifices his life for them, just as Christ gave His life for the Church. His most important responsibility as "saviour of the body" is to do everything in his power to make sure his family is rescued from the sins of the world and to eventually return to the presence of God. Paul's counsel continues:

> Therefore as the church is subject unto Christ, so let the wives be to their own husbands in every thing.
>
> Husbands, love your wives, even as Christ also loved the church, and gave himself for it;
>
> That he might sanctify and cleanse it with the washing of water by the word,
>
> That he might present it to himself a glorious church, not having spot, or wrinkle, or any such thing; but that it should be holy and without blemish. (Ephesians 5:24–27)

If a husband is fulfilling his duties in the manner in which the Lord would have him do, his wife will want to follow his direction, and he will be eager to follow her counsel as well. A vital part of the apostle Paul's counsel to the Ephesians we often miss concerning the husband-wife relationship is in the verse just before the verses that are usually discussed. There Paul teaches that husbands and wives should be "submitting yourselves *one to another* in the fear of God" (Ephesians 5:21; emphasis added). Just as the wife is to submit to her husband, so also is the husband to submit to his wife. The First Presidency and the Quorum of Twelve Apostles clearly stated in "The Family: A Proclamation to the World" that even though husbands and wives have separate roles, they are to be equal partners in carrying them out:

By divine design, fathers are to preside over their families in love and righteousness and are responsible to provide the necessities of life and protection for their families. Mothers are primarily responsible for the nurture of their children. In these sacred responsibilities, fathers and mothers are obligated to help one another as equal partners.[12]

Elder Richard G. Scott counseled priesthood holders:

As a husband and worthy priesthood bearer, you will want to emulate the example of the Savior, whose priesthood you hold. You will make giving of self to wife and children a primary focus of your life. Occasionally a man attempts to control the destiny of each family member. He makes all the decisions. His wife is subjected to his personal whims. Whether that is the custom or not is immaterial. It is not the way of the Lord. It is not the way a Latter-day Saint husband treats his wife and family.[13]

President Gordon B. Hinckley has warned men, particularly husbands and fathers, who are guilty of abuse:

No man who engages in such evil and unbecoming behavior is worthy of the priesthood of God. No man who so conducts himself is worthy of the privileges of the house of the Lord. I regret that there are some men undeserving of the love of their wives and children. There are children who fear their fathers, and wives who fear their husbands. If there be any such men within the hearing of my voice, as a servant of the Lord I rebuke you and call you to repentance. Discipline yourselves. Master your temper. Most of the things that make you angry are of very small consequence. And what a terrible price you are paying for your anger. Ask the Lord to forgive you. Ask your wife to forgive you. Apologize to your children.[14]

From "The Family: A Proclamation to the World," we read a warning not only to individuals but also to communities and nations:

We warn that individuals who violate covenants of chastity, who abuse spouse or offspring, or who fail to fulfill family responsibilities will one day stand accountable before God. Further, we warn that the disintegration of the family will bring upon individuals, communities, and nations the calamities foretold by ancient and modern prophets.[15]

RESPONSIBILITY TO THOSE WHO HAVE BEEN ABUSED

Healing from abuse is possible. Those guilty of perpetrating abuse can be forgiven by those they have abused, by God, and by the Church. Marital, family, and other relationships that have been harmed by abuse can be reconciled, but doing so is one of the most difficult challenges an individual, family, and community can face. But, as Elder Boyd K. Packer once said, "It would take a miracle, you say? Well, if it takes a miracle, why not?"[16]

Years ago during my undergraduate days at what is now Southern Utah University in Cedar City, Utah, I worked the evening shift in the emergency room at Valley View Medical Center. Late one evening during a winter snow storm, the ambulance arrived at the hospital with three members of a family who had been in an accident. A mother and her two daughters had been outside walking in the snow when they had been struck by a teenager joyriding on the icy streets in his pickup. One daughter was dead upon arrival, and the mother and the other daughter were in critical condition.

During the intense activity that accompanied their arrival at the emergency room, I asked the attending physician, a man with many years of experience, if I should call Salt Lake City and have them send a plane to transport our patients. My question wasn't out of the ordinary, because we regularly called LDS Hospital or the University of Utah Medical Center (some 250 miles distant by road) to send an airplane or a helicopter to pick up critically ill patients who were in need of care we couldn't provide in our rural hospital. The doctor's response surprised me: "Dan, what do you think we're doing here, running a first-aid station?"

He continued working, along with the other trauma team members, to do everything possible to preserve the lives of the mother and her remaining daughter, and they succeeded. The doctor later told me that our two patients would not have survived the journey to Salt Lake City had we attempted to transport them. He explained that it was the care the ambulance crew and our trauma team at the hospital gave them in the first minutes and hours following their accident that had saved their lives. During the few years I worked in the emergency room, I learned that although there were times to send our patients on to the city, there were many other times that lives could be saved if we acted quickly and wisely, using our local resources.

Victims of abuse may and often do need the sophisticated care available to them through counseling, medication, and sometimes hospitalization, but we should never fail to take seriously the healing power of the gospel of Jesus Christ, available to us in our own homes and communities. Parents and Church leaders should not underestimate their ability to assist the Savior in healing those who have been abused. President Gordon B. Hinckley has said:

> As members of the Church of Jesus Christ, ours is a ministry of healing with a duty to bind the wounds and ease the pain of those who suffer. Upon a world afflicted with greed and contention, upon families distressed by argument and selfishness, upon individuals burdened with sin and troubles and sorrows, I invoke the healing power of Christ, giving my witness of its efficacy and wonder. I testify of Him who is the great source of healing. He is the Son of God, the Redeemer of the world, the Son of Righteousness who came with healing in his wings.[17]

Abuse as a Secret Combination

Sometimes healing from abuse is complicated by people keeping secret their knowledge of abuse that has occurred and failing to share this information with those who can assist. Imagine what would have happened if the joyriding teenage driver had not reported the accident—there would have been three deaths instead of one. I don't know this, but my guess is that after the young man struck the mother and her daughters, he may have been tempted to leave the accident and by failing to report it, attempted to avoid the consequences of what he had done. There might have been a remote chance that he could have avoided the legal consequences of his actions, but the spiritual and emotional consequences of doing so would have destroyed him. Tragically, many individuals who have been abused do not talk with trustworthy adults (parents or Church leaders) because Satan has convinced them that they are the ones at fault and they will be punished. The First Presidency has clearly taught that those who have been the victims of abuse are not guilty of sin:

> Victims of rape or sexual abuse frequently experience serious trauma and unnecessary feelings of guilt. Church officers should handle such cases with sensitivity and concern, reassuring such victims that they, as victims of the evil acts of others, are not guilty of sin, helping them to overcome feelings of guilt and to regain their self-esteem and their confidence in personal relationships.
>
> Of course, a mature person who willingly consents to

sexual relations must share responsibility for the act, even though the other participant was the aggressor. Persons who consciously invite sexual advances also have a share of responsibility for the behavior that follows. But persons who are truly forced into sexual relations are victims and are not guilty of any sexual sin. . . .

Young victims of sexual abuse are likewise guilty of no sin where they are too young to be accountable for evaluating the significance of the sexual behavior. Even where acts are committed with the apparent consent of a young person, that consent may be ignored or qualified for purposes of moral responsibility where the aggressor occupied a position of authority or power over the young victim.[18]

The prophet-historian Mormon warned of the secret societies and secret acts that eventually brought the downfall of the Nephite civilization: "And behold, in the end of this book [the Book of Mormon] ye shall see that this Gadianton did prove the overthrow, yea, almost the entire destruction of the people of Nephi" (Helaman 2:13). Mormon was also warning those of us in the latter days that "secret combinations" (2 Nephi 9:9), like the ones carried out by Gadianton, could yet lead future generations to destruction, just as they did in his day.

When I ask my students to give contemporary examples of "secret combinations," invariably they describe such organizations as the Mafia, Ku Klux Klan, street gangs, and al-Qaeda. They are certainly correct in their assessments, as far as they go, but they generally have missed the idea that secret combinations could also include any "secret works of darkness" (2 Nephi 9:9), including sexual immorality, dishonesty, and abuse.

It is quite common for abuse victims to be told by their abuser, and sometimes by family and friends who know of the abuse, not to tell anyone. Sometimes such direction is given as a threat by the abuser, "for every one that doeth evil hateth the light, neither cometh to the light, lest his deeds should be reproved" (John 3:20). Individuals who have been abused and those who love them sometimes unwittingly become a part of a secret combination because they feel that bringing abuse incidents to light will only cause more harm. They fail to recognize that besides being guilty of serious sin, the abuser has committed a crime, and reporting such an infraction becomes a legal as well as a moral obligation. Bishops and branch presidents have access to legal counsel that can help Church members with unique questions related to these issues.

Share the Burden

The Book of Mormon contains a revealing account of Morianton abusing one of his maidservants and a description of her refusal to keep silent about what she had experienced: "Morianton being a man of much passion, therefore he was angry with one of his maid servants, and he fell upon her and beat her much. And it came to pass that she fled, and came over to the camp of Moroni, and told Moroni all things concerning the matter" (Alma 50:30–31).

Not only did the maidservant's report bring an end to Morianton's abuse of her but it also prevented further abuse of others by Morianton and his followers. This action of the maidservant is an important example to all who have been abused: Tell someone in authority and let him or her help. Doing so will not only provide much needed assistance to the one who has been abused but it may also prevent others from facing the same problem. Elder Richard G. Scott has counseled:

> If you are now or have in the past been abused, seek help now. Perhaps you distrust others and feel that there is no reliable help anywhere. Begin with your Eternal Father and his beloved Son, your Savior. Strive to comprehend their commandments and follow them. They will lead you to others who will strengthen and encourage you. There is available to you a priesthood leader, normally a bishop, at times a member of the stake presidency. They can build a bridge to greater understanding and healing. Joseph Smith taught: "A man can do nothing for himself unless God direct him in the right way; and the Priesthood is for that purpose." (*Teachings of the Prophet Joseph Smith,* p. 364.)[19]

Pretending the abuse did not happen, covering it up, or minimizing it is to be a part of a secret combination. Those who have been informed of the abuse are responsible to make sure the situation is dealt with in an appropriate manner. One abuse victim described her relationship with her priesthood leader as follows:

> I have been guided to priesthood leaders at various times who have been prepared to offer essential gifts in my healing. . . . My priesthood leaders have often looked scared to death as they have listened to my story and my request for assistance. But all of them listened to the Spirit and were guided in the words they spoke and the role they played.[20]

Not only can the priesthood leader provide assistance for the person who has been abused but he can also ensure that the person perpetrating the abuse receives the appropriate help as well.

"Do Not Waste Effort in Revenge"

Elder Richard G. Scott has taught: "As a victim, do not waste effort in revenge or retribution against your aggressor. Focus on your responsibility to do what is in your power to correct. Leave the handling of the offender to civil and church authorities. Whatever they do, eventually the guilty will face the Perfect Judge. Ultimately the unrepentant abuser will be punished by a just God."[21]

One common factor I have found among victims of abuse who eventually heal is that they have allowed those in authority (religious and civil) to deal with the sins of their abuser and have refrained from attempting to take justice into their own hands. In the Joseph Smith Translation, the Gospel of Luke reveals similar counsel from the Savior:

> And unto him who smiteth thee on the cheek, offer also the other; or, in other words, *it is better to offer the other, than to revile again.* And him who taketh away thy cloak, forbid not to take thy coat also.
>
> For it is better that thou suffer thine enemy to take these things, than to contend with him. *Verily I say unto you, Your heavenly Father who seeth in secret, shall bring that wicked one into judgment.*" (JST Luke 6:29–30; emphasis added)

When those who have been abused take matters into their own hands, they make it more difficult for the Lord and for Church and civil authorities to exercise justice toward those who are guilty. They also provide their abusers justification (in their own minds) for what they have done, and the persons who have been abused may cut themselves off from the much-needed influence of the Holy Ghost.

Years ago, a woman who had been sexually abused by her mother shared with me the words of the Savior that she described as having been a major part in helping her to heal from the abuse: "There is nothing from without [outside] a man, that entering into him can defile him: but the things which come out of him, those are they that defile the man" (Mark 7:15). She told me that as horrible as the abuse had been, these words of the Savior had taught her that the key to her success or failure in life wasn't what had happened to her but in how she responded to it. She discovered that what had been most destructive and had distorted her ability to feel the Lord's guidance was not the abuse but rather the hate and bitterness she felt toward her mother. Over time, as she came to understand that her feelings of hatred toward her mother and toward herself could be "swallowed up in Christ" (Mosiah 16:8), she was able to let them go and become free to experience the healing power made possible through the atonement of Christ.

Another person described her experience of recovering from abuse in a similar way:

> I am a survivor of childhood physical, emotional, and sexual abuse. I no longer view myself as a victim. The change has come from inside me—my attitude. I do not need to destroy myself with anger and hate. I don't need to entertain thoughts of revenge. My Savior knows what happened. He knows the truth. He can make the judgments and the punishments. He will be just. I will leave it in his hands. I will not be judged for what happened to me, but I will be judged by how I let it affect my life. I am responsible for my actions and what I do with my knowledge. I am not to blame for what happened to me as a child. I cannot change the past. But I can change the future. I have chosen to heal myself and pass on to my children what I have learned. The ripples in my pond will spread through future generations.[22]

Learn to Forgive

A factor shared by those who recover from abuse is the healing and liberating power of forgiveness. I often tell abuse victims, "Let me worry about *justice,* and you seek the Lord's help in preparing your heart to extend *mercy.*" Forgiveness is critical to their healing, but it is also critical to understand that it cannot be forced. A wise bishop once said, "Keep a place in your heart for forgiveness, and when it comes, welcome it in."[23]

Forgiveness is a gift of the Spirit that gradually distills upon our heart. Usually this gift follows a deliberate decision by the person who has been hurt to forgive.

The story of Joseph, son of Jacob (Israel) and Rachel, illustrates the vital place of forgiveness in the healing of those who have been abused. When Joseph was seventeen years of age, his older brothers, acting on feelings of envy because of the apparent favoritism shown to Joseph by their father, "cast him into a pit" (Genesis 37:24) and conspired to kill him. Joseph's brothers noted the "anguish of his soul" but "would not hear" (Genesis 42:21) his cries. They ended up selling him to foreign, Midianite traders for twenty pieces of silver—a third *less* than the price of a slave. Joseph was then taken by the Midianites to Egypt and purchased by Potiphar, an officer of Pharaoh.

The capture, imprisonment, and abandonment of Joseph by his brothers as well as his later enslavement were obviously forms of abuse and would have been more than most could endure, yet the writings of Moses tell us that "the Lord was with Joseph, and he was a prosperous man" (Genesis 39:2).

Feelings of anger, despair, and anxiety would be normal and probably even expected in such an ugly situation, but the phrases "the Lord was with Joseph" (Genesis 39:2) and "there is none so discreet and wise as thou art" (Genesis 41:39), as well as the miraculous success Joseph experienced, tell us that he was able to prevent such feelings from poisoning his ability to feel the comforting and directing influence of the Holy Ghost.

Two people can have the same difficult experience, and one comes out hardened and bitter; the other, softened and strengthened. From the book of Alma we read, "Because of the exceedingly great length of the war between the Nephites and the Lamanites many had become hardened, because of the exceedingly great length of the war; and many were softened because of their afflictions, insomuch that they did humble themselves before God, even in the depth of humility" (Alma 62:41).

Even after Joseph's initial success in working for Potiphar, he experienced a serious obstacle when he was sexually harassed by Potiphar's wife (Genesis 39:10). When he would not comply with her advances, she falsely accused Joseph of the very sin he was faithfully avoiding (Genesis 39:14).

Again Joseph was imprisoned and abandoned. The scriptural text describes his experience in prison with similar words from the description of his earlier imprisonment: "The Lord was with him, and that which he did, the Lord made it to prosper" (Genesis 39:23). Joseph soon found favor in the eyes of the prison officials, impressed the Pharaoh, was freed from prison, and eventually became second in command in all

Egypt. We are once again reminded of Joseph's great faith and diligence in the face of abuse and tremendous opposition.

The central lesson in the story of Joseph is the forgiveness he was able to experience and eventually extend toward his once-abusive brothers. When Joseph and his brothers finally met after twenty-two years of separation, "Joseph knew his brethren, but they knew him not" (Genesis 42:8). Eventually, "Joseph made himself known unto his brethren. And he wept aloud" (Genesis 45:1–2). The scriptural record doesn't explain why Joseph had not returned to his family once he had been able to do so years before, but that he had forgiven them is evident as the story unfolds:

> And Joseph said unto his brethren, I am Joseph; doth my father yet live? And his brethren could not answer him; for they were troubled at his presence.
>
> And Joseph said unto his brethren, Come near to me, I pray you. And they came near. And he said, I am Joseph your brother, whom ye sold into Egypt.
>
> Now therefore be not grieved, nor angry with yourselves, that ye sold me hither: for God did send me before you to preserve life. (Genesis 45:3–5)

After being reunited with his father and younger brother, Benjamin, Joseph invited Jacob and all of their other family members to come to Egypt to escape the ravages of the famine. It would have been logical for Joseph to have welcomed only Jacob and Benjamin to live with him in Egypt because they had not been a part of selling him into slavery. The scripture states, however, that "Joseph nourished his father, and his brethren, and all his father's household, with bread, according to their families" (Genesis 47:12).

After their father, Jacob, died, Joseph's brothers feared that Joseph would change his mind about the forgiveness he had graciously and mercifully extended to them. He responded to the fears of his brothers:

> And Joseph said unto them, Fear not: for am I in the place of God?
>
> But as for you, ye thought evil against me; but God meant it unto good, to bring to pass, as it is this day, to save much people alive.
>
> Now therefore fear ye not: I will nourish you, and your little ones. And he comforted them, and spake kindly unto them. (Genesis 50:19–21)

The phrase from this text, "God meant it unto good" (v. 20), should not be interpreted to mean that God had foreordained Joseph's brothers to abuse him or that the abuse Joseph experienced was something specifically designed by God. God allows us to experience evil but never foreordains the commission of evil acts. President Joseph Fielding Smith stated, "No person was foreordained or appointed to sin or to perform a mission of evil."[24] Yet the Lord does, as the Book of Mormon prophet Lehi promised his son Jacob, consecrate our afflictions for our gain:

> And behold, in thy childhood thou hast suffered afflictions and much sorrow, because of the rudeness of

thy brethren. Nevertheless, Jacob, my first-born in the wilderness, thou knowest the greatness of God; and he shall consecrate thine afflictions for thy gain.

Wherefore, thy soul shall be blessed, and thou shalt dwell safely with thy brother, Nephi; and thy days shall be spent in the service of thy God.

Wherefore, I know that thou art redeemed, because of the righteousness of thy Redeemer; for thou hast beheld that in the fulness of time he cometh to bring salvation unto men. (2 Nephi 2:1–3)

In describing Jacob's "afflictions and much sorrow" at the hands of his brothers, these words from Lehi also provide three ways in which the Lord consecrates (makes sacred) such afflictions for the blessing of his people:

1. The Lord sent Nephi as a strength to Jacob. In addition to the companionship of the Spirit of the Lord, abuse victims can also be confidant that the Lord will send "angels" both from this world and world beyond to assist them (D&C 84:88).

2. Jacob spent his days in the service of God. Church service can provide those who have suffered abuse an important opportunity of getting outside their own problems and using what they are learning to help others. As the Savior counseled, "If any man will come after me, let him deny himself, and take up his cross daily, and follow me. For whosoever will save his life shall lose it: but whosoever will lose his life for my sake, the same shall save it" (Luke 9:23–24).

3. Most important, Jacob was promised by his father that he would be "redeemed because of the righteousness of thy Redeemer" (2 Nephi 2:3). Abuse victims can be helped to cope with their problems in such a way that they can live fairly normal lives, but to truly be healed and to be completely free of the consequences of abuse requires sincere and deliberate application of the atonement of Jesus Christ. President Harold B. Lee once said:

> The greatest miracles I see today are not necessarily the healing of sick bodies, but the greatest miracles I see are the healing of sick souls, those who are sick in soul and spirit and are downhearted and distraught. . . . We are reaching out to all such, because they are precious in the sight of the Lord, and we want no one to feel that he is forgotten.[25]

CONCLUSION

Can a person who has been abused be healed? Gratefully, the answer is yes, but it is important to remember that for many it is a slow and gradual process. Elder Dallin H. Oaks, in his instructive and inspiring book *The Lord's Way*, shared important counsel and a valuable illustration. Elder Oaks stated: "One of the noblest acts of the human soul is the act of forgiveness. It can be exquisitely difficult when the wrong has been grievous, but the healing and joy that come in its wake are wonderful. Among my prized possessions are two letters from a woman who described the effects of her forgiving her older brother, who had abused her sexually when she was a child." Elder Oaks quoted from the first letter:

> The day before [regional] conference (when I was in pain from injuries received from the abuse), I had told my husband how angry I sometimes became and how sometimes I wanted to hurt my brother back for all the pain he had inflicted on me. I have tried to forgive him, but my heart wasn't totally committed to that yet.
>
> Then Sunday morning I went to conference. It seemed as if you were ready to end your talk, but the Lord prompted you to say one more thing. You said we should forgive those who had wronged us. What a witness I felt. I knew I had to forgive and LOVE my brother. And I know that only with the Lord's help can I do it, for without Him, I am nothing.
>
> The price for that sin has already been paid by Him in Gethsemane. I have no right to hold on to it and demand justice, so I gladly hand it back to Him and rejoice in His love and mercy. . . . My heart is so full of joy, peace and gratitude and love! Isn't His work glorious? How I do love Him! Words cannot express my feelings.

Elder Oaks then described the second letter he received from this sister:

> I replied, and a week later I received a second letter, describing what followed her change of heart. "The day I received your letter I felt the healing process was

completed for me," she wrote, "and I was filled with charity for my brother." The next day she received word that her brother, a less-active member of the Church who lived in another state, had been hospitalized with serious injury. She immediately phoned and asked a friend to give him a priesthood blessing. In that blessing he was told that his sister loved him.

The next night, while he was on support systems, hovering between life and death, she felt his spirit in her home and was able to feel his realization of the horror of what he had done to her and to others. She felt his remorse and his desire to repent, and she felt that she was able to communicate with him. The next day he died.

She wrote me: "I feel such mercy from the Lord, realizing that [my brother] just wasn't quite strong enough to right his life here. And I plead for mercy that the price he has to pay will not be too harsh. . . . I love the Lord so much. Being a convert to the Church, it is so sweet to feel His love. I can never express my gratitude to Him adequately. I marvel at His ways and His love and mercy."[26]

Bad things don't happen only to good people, or to bad people, or to those of us in between. They happen to *all* people. How very blessed we are to have a Savior who has been sent "to heal the brokenhearted, to preach deliverance to the captives, and recovering of sight to the blind, to set at liberty them that are bruised" (Luke 4:18; see also Isaiah 61:1–2).

CHAPTER SEVEN

Is It Possible to Reconcile War with the Teachings of Jesus Christ?

Several years ago I attended a lecture where a fellow professor quoted from President David O. McKay as a part of an argument against America going to war in a foreign land:

In the face of the tragic condition among mankind, honest thinking men and women ask how is it possible to reconcile the teachings of Jesus with the participation of the Church in armed conflict.

War is basically selfish. Its roots feed in the soil of envy, hatred, desire for domination. Its fruit, therefore, is always bitter. They who cultivate and propagate it spread death and destruction, and are enemies of the human race.

War originates in the hearts of men who seek to despoil, to conquer, or to destroy other individuals or groups of individuals. Self exaltation is a motivating factor; force, the means of attainment. War is rebellious action against moral order.

The present war [World War II] had its beginning in militarism, a false philosophy which believes that "war is a biological necessity for the purification and progress of nations." It proclaims that Might determines Right, and that only the strongest nations should survive and rule. It says, "the grandeur of history lies in the perpetual conflict of nations, and it is simply foolish to desire the suppression of their rivalry."

War impels you to hate your enemies.

The Prince of Peace says, Love your enemies.

War says, Curse them that curse you.

The Prince of Peace says, Pray for them that curse you.

War says, Injure and kill them that hate you.

The Risen Lord says, Do good to them that hate you.

Thus we see that war is incompatible with Christ's teachings. The gospel of Jesus Christ is the gospel of peace. War is its antithesis, and produces hate. It is vain to attempt to reconcile war with true Christianity.[1]

I can still recall the feelings of surprise I experienced as I heard this professor read President McKay's words, for they appeared to contradict what I had previously been taught and had read from the scriptures about war being justified in some circumstances. The professor went on to criticize our national leaders, specifically the currently serving president of the United States for his decision to place American soldiers in a foreign land. Because of my confusion and because what the professor had read was only part of President McKay's address, I was anxious to read the general conference talk in its entirety. I was questioning myself about whether this was one of those situations where modern prophets had spoken and I hadn't had "ears to hear" (Luke 14:35).

When I read the complete manuscript of President McKay's talk, however, I found that the professor had indeed quoted him accurately—but only to a certain point. What the professor had failed to do was to complete President McKay's discussion of war. Following are the words of President McKay the professor did not include in his presentation:

> In the face of all this I shall seem inconsistent when I declare that I uphold our country in the gigantic task it has assumed in the present world conflict [World War II], and sustain the Church in its loyal support of the government in its fight against dictatorship. . . .
>
> . . . I still say that there are conditions when entrance into war is justifiable, and when a Christian nation may, without violation of principles, take up arms against an opposing force.
>
> Such a condition, however, is not a real or fancied insult given by one nation to another. When this occurs proper reparation may be made by mutual understanding, apology, or by arbitration.
>
> Neither is there justifiable cause found in a desire or even a need for territorial expansion. The taking of territory implies the subjugation of the weak by the strong—the application of the jungle law.

Nor is war justified in an attempt to enforce a new order of government, or even to impel others to a particular form of worship, however better the government or eternally true the principles of the enforced religion may be.

There are, however, two conditions which may justify a truly Christian man to enter—mind you, I say *enter, not begin*—a war: (1) An attempt to dominate and to deprive another of his free agency, and, (2) Loyalty to his country. Possibly there is a third, viz., Defense of a weak nation that is being unjustly crushed by a strong, ruthless one.[2]

My experience with this professor illustrates some of the confusion that exists among many Latter-day Saints concerning the question of war. Many who discuss the morality of war select only a few passages from scripture or from the teachings of our leaders that support their own (usually political) bias. It is possible that some have quoted the second half of President McKay's talk on the necessity of war, leaving out the first part about the Savior's teachings on peace—just the reverse of what my professor friend had done. Each is as much a distortion of the truth as the other. While the Lord, acting through the First Presidency, has encouraged us to be active in the political party of our choice, it is critical that we understand and be true to the Lord's perspective on war and the various other issues we face, as reflected in His doctrines, principles, and practices. President Harold B. Lee once stated:

You may not like what comes from the authority of the Church. It may contradict your political views. It may contradict your social views. It may interfere with some of your social life. But if you listen to these things, as if from the mouth of the Lord himself, with patience and faith, the promise is that "the gates of hell shall not prevail against you; yea, and the Lord God will disperse the powers of darkness from before you, and cause the heavens to shake for your good, and his name's glory." (D&C 21:6.)[3]

There is no lasting peace nor safety in embracing and promoting personal agendas not in genuine harmony with the Savior's teachings. Sadly, some of the most divisive discussions many of us have witnessed have been in Sunday School, priesthood meeting, or Relief Society, where individuals distort the teachings of the Lord and His servants as a means of giving voice to their own political perspectives. Although there are appropriate times and places in which one's own political opinions may be expressed, religious settings where the doctrines of Christ are to be taught are not among them. We should study the Savior's teachings on war, along with the teachings of His servants, both ancient and modern, so that we may be true to what the Lord has revealed concerning this difficult subject.

PEACE HAS BEEN TAKEN FROM THE EARTH

As Christians we are sometimes deceived into believing that the Savior's teachings are restricted to the doctrines of love and mercy, forgetting that God's *justice* is as equally an expression of His love as is His mercy. Christian philosopher C. S. Lewis wrote: "Mercy, detached from Justice, grows unmerciful. That is the important paradox. As there are plants which will flourish only in mountain soil, so it appears that Mercy will flower only when it grows in the crannies of the rock of Justice."[4] The prophet Alma taught his son Corianton, "What, do ye suppose that mercy can rob justice? I say unto you, Nay; not one whit. If so, God would cease to be God" (Alma 42:25).

Conversely, there are those among us who misinterpret the Savior's teachings about justice and personal responsibility to the exclusion of His *mercy*, forgetting that in addition to being perfectly just, God is also perfectly forgiving and kind. The Savior's teachings on war are an awe-inspiring expression of the "perfect balance" of His character and perfections, especially His attributes of justice and mercy. President Ezra Taft Benson has stated:

> Nearly two thousand years ago a perfect Man walked the earth—Jesus the Christ. He was the Son of a Heavenly Father and an earthly mother. He is the God of this world, under the Father. In His life, all the virtues were lived and kept in *perfect balance;* He taught men truth—that they might be free; His example and precepts provide the great standard—the only sure way—for all mankind.[5]

The continuing debates over war in various parts of the earth, particularly since the events in the United States on

September 11, 2001, are tragic reminders of the prophecies concerning "wars and rumors of wars" described throughout scripture (Matthew 24:6, Mark 13:7, 1 Nephi 12:2, 21; 14:15–16; 2 Nephi 25:12; D&C 45:26; Joseph Smith–Matthew 1:28). The many conflicts in which the world is now engaged remind us of the sobering reality that the future will not be free from war, terror, death, and destruction. The words of prophets in all ages indicate that such conflicts will continue until the second coming of Jesus Christ and will also be experienced one last time after the Savior's millennial reign (Revelation 20:7–8). Elder Bruce R. McConkie stated:

> Be it remembered that tribulations lie ahead. There will be wars in one nation and kingdom after another until war is poured out upon all nations and two hundred million men of war mass their armaments at Armageddon.
>
> Peace has been taken from the earth, the angels of destruction have begun their work, and their swords shall not be sheathed until the Prince of Peace comes to destroy the wicked and usher in the great Millennium. . . .
>
> It is one of the sad heresies of our time that peace will be gained by weary diplomats as they prepare treaties of compromise, or that the Millennium will be ushered in because men will learn to live in peace and to keep the commandments, or that the predicted plagues and promised desolations of latter days can in some way be avoided. We must do all we can to proclaim peace, to avoid war, to heal disease, to prepare for natural disasters—but with it all, that which is to be shall be.[6]

On November 1, 1831, the Lord revealed through the Prophet Joseph Smith that "the day speedily cometh; the hour is not yet, but is nigh at hand, *when peace shall be taken from the earth*" (D&C 1:35; emphasis added). In April 1937 Elder Joseph Fielding Smith acknowledged that this dreaded day had indeed arrived:

> One year after the organization of the Church, peace could not have been taken from the earth, in justice, but the Lord said the time would speedily come. That time has come. Peace has departed from the world. The devil has power today over his own dominion. This is made manifest in the actions of men, in the distress among the nations, in the troubles that we see in all lands, including this land which was dedicated to liberty.[7]

THE LORD'S LAW OF WAR

While we have been commanded by the Lord to "renounce war and proclaim peace" (D&C 98:16), the Lord and His servants have also instructed us that from time to time we as individuals and as nations are justified in going to war for the protection of the innocent and the establishment of peace. In April 2003 President Gordon B. Hinckley reminded the members of the Church, "It is clear from these [teachings of the Book of Mormon] and other writings that there are times and circumstances when nations are justified, in fact have an obligation, to fight for family, for liberty, and against tyranny, threat, and oppression."[8]

COUNSEL ON WAR FROM THE BOOK OF MORMON

To me it is no coincidence, and indeed a great blessing, that the Book of Mormon contains so much detail concerning war. The prophet Moroni was speaking of our day when he recorded, "Behold, the Lord hath shown unto me great and marvelous things concerning that which must shortly come, at that day when these things [the Book of Mormon records] shall come forth among you. Behold, I speak unto you as if ye were present, and yet ye are not. But behold, Jesus Christ hath shown you unto me, and I know your doing" (Mormon 8:34–35).

Certainly some of what Moroni saw in vision and recorded for us to study were the ever-present wars and contentions in which the world is presently engaged. Not only do we read of the events surrounding the many wars that plagued the ancient inhabitants of the Americas, but as President Ezra Taft Benson taught, "From the Book of Mormon we learn how disciples of Christ live in times of war."[9]

From the beginning the Book of Mormon provides detailed descriptions of the tragedies and evils of war. Despite Nephi's faithful efforts to promote peace with his brothers Laman and Lemuel, he was not able to reconcile the serious differences that existed between them. Finally he was commanded by the Lord to "depart from them and flee into the wilderness" (2 Nephi 5:5). Nephi was directed by the Lord to craft swords for the protection of his people because their lives were constantly in jeopardy (2 Nephi 5:14). Wars and contentions between the Nephites and Lamanites continued almost constantly from the time Nephi was commanded to depart from his brothers, sometime between 580 and 570 B.C., until the coming of the resurrected Savior many generations later (Enos; Omni; Mosiah 19–23; Alma 2–3, 16, 24–25, 28, 43–62; Helaman 1–4, 6, 10–11; 3 Nephi 1–4, 6–7).

Even though the Nephites obtained the Jaredite record, which chronicled their destruction by war (Ether 7–11, 13–15), it did not divert Lehi's descendants from their own march to annihilation. Peace prevailed for some two hundred years after the Savior ministered among the people, but from that point forward, the scriptural record is again rife with tension, war, and repeated violence between and among the Nephites and the Lamanites (Mormon 1–6; Moroni 9). In fact, nearly a quarter of the 249 chapters in the Book of Mormon discuss some aspect of physical warfare.

Have Righteous Intent

One detailed example of a "just war" in the Book of Mormon is the battle between Captain Moroni's forces and the Lamanite army led by Zerahemnah. Mormon's account contains many valuable lessons concerning what is sometimes called "the Lord's law of war." The prophet-historian Mormon described Captain Moroni's understanding of the differences in motive that existed between the Nephite and the Lamanite forces:

Moroni knew the intention of the Lamanites, that it was their intention to destroy their brethren, or to subject them and bring into bondage that they might establish a kingdom unto themselves over all the land. And he also knowing that it was the only desire of the Nephites to preserve their lands, and their liberty, and their church, therefore he thought it no sin that he should defend them by stratagem. (Alma 43:30)

In addition to understanding the importance of righteous motives, Moroni understood that the Lord's law of war meant that to be justified in going to war, he and his armies could not initiate conflict. The Lord taught them, "Inasmuch as ye are not guilty of the first offense, neither the second, ye shall not suffer yourselves to be slain by the hands of your enemies" (Alma 43:46).

Seek the Lord's Consent

Another important principle of waging a just war is found in the example of Moroni seeking the Lord's consent and direction through the prophet Alma before going to war against the Lamanites. From the book of Alma we read, "Moroni, also, knowing of the prophecies of Alma, sent certain men unto him, desiring him that he should inquire of the Lord whither the armies of the Nephites should go to defend themselves against the Lamanites" (Alma 43:23). Though history documents that some religious leaders have given counsel to their followers contrary to the will of the Lord and that leaders of nations have sometimes chosen the wrong path, generally presidents of the United States of America have sought counsel from the nation's religious leaders concerning matters of international conflict. President Gordon B. Hinckley was among a group of religious leaders from across the nation who were called upon by President George W. Bush to assist him regarding America's response to terrorism and decisions concerning war.[10]

The Doctrine and Covenants provides a second witness of the principle of seeking the Lord's approval to go to war. The Lord counseled the Prophet Joseph Smith, "Behold, this is the law I gave unto my servant Nephi, and thy fathers, Joseph, and Jacob, and Isaac, and Abraham, and all mine ancient prophets and apostles . . . that they should not go out unto battle against any nation, kindred, tongue, or people, save I, the Lord, commanded them" (D&C 98:32–33).

In Moroni's case the Lord gave His consent through the prophet Alma, and "the work of death commenced on both sides, but it was more dreadful on the part of the Lamanites" (Alma 43:37). Mormon tells us that as the war between the Nephites and the Lamanites progressed, the Lamanites "did fight like dragons, and many of the Nephites were slain by their hands" (Alma 43:44). The Book of Mormon further reveals, "The Lord suffereth the righteous to be slain that his justice and judgment may come upon the wicked" (Alma 60:13; see also 14:11), but the Lord has also promised that "he will not suffer that the wicked shall destroy the righteous" (1 Nephi 22:16). Many righteous soldiers and civilians have died on all sides of the various wars the world has witnessed, but the Lord's promise is that as a group the righteous will be preserved.

Obey Righteous Counsel

A significant example of obedience to the counsel of the Lord, as well as additional insights concerning the principles upon which a just war is based, is found in the Book of Mormon account of Nephi obtaining the plates of brass. As Nephi entered Jerusalem and went towards the house of Laban to obtain the records, he "beheld a man, and he had fallen to the earth . . . , for he was drunken with wine" (1 Nephi 4:7). Soon after realizing that the drunken man was Laban, Nephi was "constrained by the Spirit that [he] should kill Laban" (1 Nephi 4:10).

Nephi's first response to the Spirit's direction was, "Never at any time have I shed the blood of man" (1 Nephi 4:10)—reflective of his reverence for the commandment "Thou shalt not kill" (Exodus 20:13) and his regard for the sanctity of life. But after detailing the reasons why the taking of Laban's life was justified, the Spirit instructed Nephi further: "Slay him, for the Lord hath delivered him into thy hands" (1 Nephi 4:12). Difficult as it was to do, Nephi obeyed the Lord's command and thus preserved the spiritual lives of the family of Lehi and of generations yet unborn. As Nephi declared, "Behold the Lord slayeth the wicked to bring forth his righteous purposes. It is better that one man should perish than that a nation should dwindle and perish in unbelief" (1 Nephi 4:13).

In contrast, the lives of innocent people may be lost because of the refusal of their leaders to follow inspired counsel. One of most tragic stories in the history of the Church is the tragedy at Haun's Mill. In the fall of 1838, the Prophet Joseph Smith counseled all of the Latter-day Saints scattered across northern Missouri to move to Far West for protection. The Prophet Joseph specifically warned Jacob Haun, the founder of the settlement, to warn the people who were living at Haun's Mill to move into Far West. Jacob Haun failed to warn the people, and many innocent people—men, women, and children—lost their lives. After reviewing the historical details of the tragic events surrounding the events at Haun's Mill, Elder Henry B. Eyring provided an additional key as to how we may better identify and follow the Lord's counsel concerning the various challenges we face:

> In our own time, we have been warned with counsel of where to find safety from sin and from sorrow. One of the keys to recognizing those warnings is that they are repeated. For instance, more than once in these general conferences, you have heard our prophet say that he would quote a preceding prophet and would therefore be a second witness and sometimes even a third. . . . When the words of prophets seem repetitive, that should rivet our attention and fill our hearts with gratitude to live in such a blessed time.[11]

Much of the counsel concerning war that we find in scripture and in the words of living prophets has been repeated many times and in many different settings.

Seek Reconciliation

Mormon, who named his own son Moroni, included the account of Captain Moroni's attempts at negotiating a peace agreement with Zerahemnah and his followers. Besides demanding that Zerahemnah "deliver up your weapons of war unto us" (Alma 44:6), Moroni insisted that Zerahemnah and his people covenant that they would not resume the battle against the Nephites at a later time: "Therefore as the Lord liveth, ye shall not depart except ye depart with an oath that ye will not return again against us to war. Now as ye are in our hands we will spill your blood upon the ground, or ye shall submit to the conditions which I have proposed" (Alma 44:11). Some refused and were killed; others entered into "a covenant of peace" and were spared (Alma 44:15).

Doctrine and Covenants 98 provides additional detail concerning the process of first seeking reconciliation through negotiation before resorting to war:

> And if any nation, tongue, or people should proclaim war against them, they should first lift a standard of peace unto that people, nation, or tongue;
>
> And if that people did not accept the offering of peace, neither the second nor the third time, they should bring these testimonies before the Lord;

Then I, the Lord, would give unto them a commandment, and justify them in going out to battle
against that nation, tongue, or people. (D&C 98:34–36)

Maintain Personal Righteousness

Moroni explained to Zerahemnah that the most important
reason why the Nephites would eventually prevail in their war
with the Lamanites was their personal obedience to the commandments of God: "Now ye see that . . . God will support,
and keep, and preserve us, so long as we are faithful unto him,
and unto our faith, and our religion; and never will the Lord
suffer that we shall be destroyed except we should fall into
transgression and deny our faith" (Alma 44:4).

President Gordon B. Hinckley gave similar counsel to the
members of the Church in our day soon after the terrorist
attacks of September 11, 2001: "God our Eternal Father will
watch over this nation and all of the civilized world who look
to Him. He has declared, 'Blessed is the nation whose God is
the Lord' (Ps. 33:12). Our safety lies in repentance. Our
strength comes of obedience to the commandments of God."[12]
It may appear that there is little we can do individually to promote peace in the nations of the world that are at war, but we
can live worthy of the companionship of the Holy Ghost and
strive to live peacefully with our own family, friends, and
neighbors. President Hinckley has also stated:

There is much of another category of sickness among
us. I speak of conflicts, quarrels, arguments which are a

debilitating disease particularly afflicting families. If there be such problems in the homes of any within the sound of my voice, I encourage you to invite the healing power of Christ. To those to whom He spoke on the Mount, Jesus said: "Ye have heard that it hath been said, An eye for an eye, and a tooth for a tooth:

"But I say unto you, That ye resist not evil: but whosoever shall smite thee on thy right cheek, turn to him the other also. . . .

"And whosoever shall compel thee to go a mile, go with him twain." (Matt. 5:38–41.)

The application of this principle, difficult to live but wondrous in its curative powers, would have a miraculous effect on our troubled homes. It is selfishness which is the cause of most of our misery. It is as a cankering disease. The healing power of Christ, found in the doctrine of going the second mile, would do wonders to still argument and accusation, fault-finding and evil speaking.[13]

COUNSEL ON WAR FROM THE OLD TESTAMENT

One of the many scriptural examples of the Lord's justification of war is in the familiar Old Testament account of the conflict between the children of Israel and the Pharaoh of Egypt and his army. As Moses led the Israelites out of Egypt towards the promised land, the Israelite people expressed their fear that they would be recaptured or destroyed by Pharaoh and his mighty army. Moses responded to their anxiety by encouraging them to have faith in the Lord: "Fear ye not, stand still, and see the salvation of the Lord, which he will shew to you to day: for the Egyptians whom ye have seen to day, ye shall see them again no more for ever. The Lord shall fight for you, and ye shall hold your peace" (Exodus 14:13–14). We then read of the Lord directing Moses to lead the Israelites to safety and causing the Egyptians to be drowned in the depths of the Red Sea.

After the Israelites realized that their lives had been preserved and that God had miraculously kept them from destruction, a hymn of rejoicing and gratitude was composed and sung that included the words "The Lord is a man of war" (Exodus 15:3). One of the lost books of ancient Israel, "the book of the wars of the Lord" (Numbers 21:14), apparently included many such songs sung by the Israelites as a part of their worship and celebration following the righteous conquest of their enemies. The Old Testament contains many accounts of the Lord fighting the battles of His people and justifying their participation in war.

Reverence Life

In counsel that was intended to include the sanctity even of animal life, the Lord stated, "The blood of every beast will I require at your hands" (JST Genesis 9:11).

> For, behold, the beasts of the field and the fowls of the air, and that which cometh of the earth, is ordained

for the use of man for food and for raiment, and that he might have in abundance.

But it is not given that one man should possess that which is above another, wherefore the world lieth in sin.

And wo be unto man that sheddeth blood or that wasteth flesh and hath no need (D&C 49:19–21).

The Prophet Joseph Smith taught, "I exhorted the brethren not to kill the serpent, bird, or an animal of any kind during our journey unless it became necessary in order to preserve ourselves from hunger."[14]

The Joseph Smith Translation of the Bible, the Book of Mormon, and the Doctrine and Covenants all read, "Thou shalt not kill" when referring to the Sixth Commandment (JST Exodus 20:13; Mosiah 13:21; 3 Nephi 12:21; D&C 132:36). "Thou shalt not kill" is an appropriate and absolute warning to everyone that all life is sacred. In our own day, the First Presidency and the Quorum of the Twelve have "affirm[ed] the sanctity of life and of its importance in God's eternal plan."[15]

Remember That Murder Is Never Justified

One of the difficulties some individuals have in reconciling the legitimacy of war and the taking of life is the Sixth of the Ten Commandments: "Thou shalt not kill" (Exodus 20:13). Paradoxically, the Lord also said to Moses, "Thou shalt utterly destroy" (Deuteronomy 20:17). The words of the Prophet Joseph Smith give us some understanding of why the Lord gave what appear to be contradictory commandments:

That which is wrong under one circumstance, may be, and often is, right under another. God said, "Thou shalt not kill;" at another time He said, "Thou shalt utterly destroy." This is the principle on which the government of heaven is conducted—by revelation adapted to the circumstances in which the children of the kingdom are placed. Whatever God requires is right, no matter what it is, although we may not see the reason thereof till long after the events transpire.[16]

The teachings of the prophets throughout all dispensations confirm that no matter the circumstance, obedience to God is paramount. The Old Testament clearly teaches that at times God may require and authorize the taking of life; on other occasions He may command that life be preserved. Murder, the unauthorized taking of life, involves a selfish motive and often a criminal intent. Murder is always wrong under any circumstance, at any time, by any person. We can be assured that though we too may be faced with "a time to kill, and a time to heal. . . . a time of war, and a time of peace" (Ecclesiastes 3:3, 8), the Lord through His servants and through the influence of the Holy Ghost will assist us in making the difficult decisions we may be called upon to make.

COUNSEL ON WAR FROM THE NEW TESTAMENT

Jesus Christ clearly taught, "Ye have heard that it hath been said, An eye for an eye, and a tooth for a tooth: But I say unto you, That ye *resist not evil:* but whosoever shall smite thee on thy right cheek, turn to him the other also" (Matthew 5:38–39; emphasis added; see also 3 Nephi 12:38–39). There are many injustices the Lord would have us simply let go and forget. Elder Dallin H. Oaks, in his remarkable book *The Lord's Way,* shares the following insight from a colleague illustrating the meaning of the phrase "resist not evil" (Matthew 5:39):

> In a stimulating analysis of the application of this commandment [resist not evil] in the circumstances of our day, Leonard E. Read, the long-time editor of *The Freeman,* concluded that it meant "not to argue with anyone. . . . In a word, away with confrontation!" He gave this illustration: "Now and then we experience shysterism: a broken promise, overcharge, underquality, an attempt to 'get the best' of one. Resist not this evil; that is, pay no heed; not a scolding word; simply walk away and fail to return. While resistance will harden the malefactor in his sins as he rises to his own defense, nonresistance leaves him alone with his soul, his shop, and his jobbery, a plight even a malefactor will ponder and understand."[17]

Many individuals, such as those who take an absolute stand against military conflict of any kind, interpret the Savior's command "resist not evil" (Matthew 5:39) to mean that we should never actively resist evil in any way at any time. Such a perspective is supported by several other texts as well, including counsel from the Savior: "Ye have heard that it hath been said by them of old time, and it is also written before you, that thou shalt not kill, and whosoever shall kill shall be in danger of the judgment of God; but I say unto you, that whosoever is angry with his brother shall be in danger of his judgment" (3 Nephi 12:21–22; see also JST Matthew 5:21–22).

This counsel from the Savior clearly indicates that while the law of Moses held individuals to the standard of not taking another's life unjustly, His higher law commands us not even to be angry! Those who believe war is never justified ask how it is possible to live to such a high standard and still take part in armed conflict.

Receive Authorization

Invitations to "resist not evil" (Matthew 5:39) and to avoid anger are especially challenging when reading the accounts of the great military leaders in the Book of Mormon. One of the unsung heroes of the Book of Mormon, the chief judge Pahoran, counseled his chief captain, Moroni:

> Therefore, my beloved brother, Moroni, let us *resist evil,* and whatsoever evil we cannot resist with our words, yea, such as rebellions and dissensions, *let us resist them with our swords,* that we may retain our freedom, that we may rejoice in the great privilege of our church, and in the cause of our Redeemer and our God. (Alma 61:14; emphasis added)

Although some scholars appropriately explain this apparent contradiction between the words of the Savior and the words of Pahoran by explaining the differences between the lesser law of Moses and the higher law of Christ, I believe the scriptures provide an additional answer. This scriptural insight sheds light on both the question concerning war and the problems we face with interpersonal conflicts as well.

In the verse of scripture that follows the counsel from Pahoran to "resist evil" (Alma 61:14), the answer to the apparent contradiction begins to unfold. Pahoran wrote to Moroni:

> Therefore, come unto me speedily with a few of your men, and leave the remainder in the charge of Lehi and Teancum; *give unto them power to conduct the war* in that part of the land, according to the Spirit of God, which is also the spirit of freedom which is in them. (Alma 61:15; emphasis added)

Pahoran was reviewing with Moroni the necessity of *authorizing* his men to conduct the affairs of war, which would obviously include the taking of life. In and of themselves, Moroni's soldiers did not have the right to wage war as a group or individually without formal authorization. Though the Lord always wants us to "resist the devil" (James 4:7) by avoiding sin, we should not formally "resist evil" (Alma 61:14) by waging war without the proper authorization. When Jesus stated, "Resist not evil" (Matthew 5:39; 3 Nephi 12:39) to His followers in both Jerusalem and the Americas, He was speaking to them in connection with their day-to-day, personal relationships. Moroni's charge from Pahoran to "resist evil" (Alma 61:14) was in regard to their authorized duties as agents of the Nephite government and as servants of the Lord.

Leave Justice to the Lord and His Servants

The New Testament also provides important details concerning when we are to formally resist evil and when we are not. In a classic discourse on retaliation and revenge, the apostle Paul counseled:

> Recompense to no man evil for evil. Provide things honest in the sight of all men.
>
> If it be possible, as much as lieth in you, live peaceably with all men.
>
> Dearly beloved, *avenge not yourselves, but rather give [God] place unto wrath: for it is written, Vengeance is mine; I will repay, saith the Lord.*
>
> Therefore if thine enemy hunger, feed him; if he thirst, give him drink: for in so doing thou shalt heap coals of fire on his head.
>
> Be not overcome of evil, but overcome evil with good. (Romans 12:17–21; emphasis added)

Paul explained that it is our individual responsibility to exercise *mercy* towards those who have offended us, and we are to leave *justice* to God and to His authorized servants. The scriptures teach, "Be ye therefore merciful, as your Father also is merciful" (Luke 6:36) and allow "God to recompense tribulation to them that trouble you" (2 Thessalonians 1:6). When we take matters into our own hands and seek justice on our own terms, we make things worse for ourselves, for those who have offended us, and for those who are attempting to bring about a peaceful resolution. Notice the doctrinal detail in the following verses from the Joseph Smith Translation as the Savior warns against retaliation and also counsel us to leave judgment to Him:

> And unto him who smiteth thee on the cheek, offer also the other; or, in other words, *it is better to offer the other, than to revile again.* And him who taketh away thy cloak, forbid not to take thy coat also.
>
> For it is better that thou suffer thine enemy to take these things, than to contend with him. *Verily I say unto you, Your heavenly Father who seeth in secret, shall bring that wicked one into judgment.* (JST Luke 6:29–30; emphasis added)

The scriptures also teach that the Lord will sometimes use civil authority to punish the wicked. The apostle Peter taught the early Saints the importance of submitting themselves to civil authority and allowing the Lord's use of the government to bring the wicked to judgment: "Submit yourselves to every ordinance of man for the Lord's sake: whether it be to the king, as supreme; or unto governors, as unto them *that are sent by him for the punishment of evildoers*" (1 Peter 2:13–17; emphasis added; see also D&C 134:1).

Just as religious leaders have a solemn responsibility to mete out justice on behalf of the Church to those guilty of sin, and parents have the authority to discipline their children, civil authorities are also responsible to maintain order and appropriately deal with those who have broken the law.

Writing of both civil and religious leaders, the apostle Paul taught:

> For rulers are not a terror to good works, but to the evil. Wilt thou then not be afraid of the power? do that which is good, and thou shalt have praise of the same:
>
> For he is the minister of God to thee for good. But if thou do that which is evil, be afraid; for he beareth not the sword in vain: for he is the minister of God, a revenger to *execute* wrath upon him that doeth evil. (Romans 13:3–4)

The Old Testament contains several examples of the Lord carrying out justice by the hand of civil governments. He used the king of the Medes to bring the Babylonians to justice (Jeremiah 51:11), and when Edom needed to be disciplined the Lord stated, "I will lay my vengeance upon Edom by the hand of my people Israel" (Ezekiel 25:14).

Likewise, in the Book of Mormon, the prophet Nephi was warned by the Lord that the Lamanites would be a "scourge unto thy seed, to stir them up in remembrance of me; and inasmuch as they will not remember me, and hearken unto my words, they shall scourge them even unto destruction" (2 Nephi 5:25; see also Mormon 5:22–24).

It is a normal human desire to punish those who have sinned against us. In addition to being angry with them, we also fear that if we don't punish them, no one else will. The problem with this reasoning is that as we nurture our feelings of anger and harbor the desire for others to be punished, we will lose the comforting and directing influence of the Holy Ghost in our own lives. The Lord has counseled, "To me belongeth vengeance, and recompence; their foot shall slide in due time: for the day of their calamity is at hand, and the things that shall come upon them make haste" (Deuteronomy 32:35).

By seeking to carry out justice ourselves, we interfere with the Lord and His servants in carrying out the process His way and according to His timetable. It is important to remember that justice belongs to God and His authorized servants, civil and religious. It is our duty to exercise mercy. It is to be hoped that we can treat our enemies as David responded to Saul, "The Lord judge between me and thee, and the Lord avenge me of thee: but mine hand shall not be upon thee" (1 Samuel 24:12).

CONCLUSION

Is it possible to reconcile war with the teachings of Jesus Christ? The answer is a qualified yes. Our prophets have clearly taught that war is sometimes necessary to bring about peace and that in some cases, without just war, chaos and evil would reign.

Several years ago I had the privilege of speaking to members of the Church in Belfast, Northern Ireland. As I entered the chapel and was seated on the stand before the meeting began, I observed several uniformed men entering the chapel. From the way they greeted the other people in attendance and from the scriptures in their hands, it was obvious that they were members of the Church. I mentioned to the presiding authority sitting next to me how wonderful it must be to have members of the Church serving in the local police force and that their influence must certainly be a part of the solution to the conflict in Northern Ireland.

He acknowledged their goodness and the good work they were doing, but then he made a statement that put the conflict in Northern Ireland in an eternal context. "Brother Judd," he said, "they certainly are good men and they do much good, but as good as they are, the real answer to our problems in Northern Ireland are seated over there." He pointed toward the full-time missionaries. As I watched those wonderful missionaries, young and old, interact with each other and with the investigators they had brought to the meeting, I thought of the words of the Savior: "Blessed are the peacemakers: for they shall be called the children of God" (Matthew 5:9). These words from "the Prince of Peace" (Isaiah 9:6) remind us that it is the gospel of Jesus Christ that will eventually bring lasting peace to Northern Ireland and to all the world.

CHAPTER EIGHT

How Can We Find Peace amidst Adversity?

A mong the lessons we learn from the lives and teachings of the prophets is the importance of facing the hard questions and challenges of life with a spirit of hope and optimism. The scriptures and the recorded history of the Church are well supplied with examples of men, women, and, in some cases, children who learned to place their faith in Jesus Christ and follow His example, even in the most trying of circumstances. In the Gospel of John, we read the words of the Savior concerning the means by which hope and peace are made possible to all who have ears to hear: "These things I have spoken unto you, that *in me ye might have peace*. In the world ye shall have tribulation: but be of good cheer; I have overcome the world" (John 16:33; emphasis added).

Although there are many temporary strategies for finding peace amidst adversity, the only way to experience the "peace of God, which passeth all understanding" (Philippians 4:7) is through the "merits, and mercy, and grace of the Holy

Messiah" (2 Nephi 2:8). The counsel of the Savior and of prophets ancient and modern points us to what the Lord described as "the covenant of my peace" (3 Nephi 22:10), which nurtures a spirit of optimism, inspires hope, increases faith, strengthens families, and helps maintain or reclaim sanity in the lives of those who face hard questions and seek to implement the answers the Lord has provided.

THE EXAMPLES AND TEACHINGS OF LATTER-DAY PROPHETS

In the face of nearly constant opposition and adversity, the Prophet Joseph Smith maintained what is described in the Pearl of Great Price as his "native cheery temperament" (Joseph Smith–History 1:28). The Prophet's optimism amidst adversity is evident in an entry from his journal reflecting on the challenges he was facing with his family and his leadership responsibilities in the Church:

> *Friday Morning, January 1, 1836.*—This being the beginning of a new year, my heart is filled with gratitude to God that He has preserved my life, and the lives of my family, while another year has passed away. We have been sustained and upheld in the midst of a wicked and perverse generation, although exposed to all the afflictions, temptations, and misery that are incident to human life; for this I feel to humble myself in dust and ashes, as it were, before the Lord. But notwithstanding the gratitude that fills my heart on retrospecting the past year, and the

multiplied blessings that have crowned our heads, my heart is pained within me, because of the difficulty that exists in my father's family. The devil has made a violent attack on my brother William and Calvin Stoddard, and the powers of darkness seem to lower over their minds, and not only over theirs, but they also cast a gloomy shade over the minds of my brethren and sisters, which prevents them from seeing things as they really are; and the powers of earth and hell seem combined to overthrow us and the Church, by causing a division in the family; and indeed the adversary is bringing into requisition all his subtlety to prevent the Saints from being endowed, by causing a division among the Twelve, also among the Seventy, and bickering and jealousies among the Elders and the official members of the Church; and so the leaven of iniquity ferments and spreads among the members of the Church. But I am determined that nothing on my part shall be lacking to adjust and amicably dispose of and settle all family difficulties on this day, that the ensuing year and years, be they few or many, may be spent in righteousness before God. And I know that the cloud will burst, and Satan's kingdom be laid in ruins, with all his black designs; and that the Saints will come forth like gold seven times tried in the fire, being made perfect through sufferings and temptations, and that the blessings of heaven and earth will be multiplied upon their heads; which may God grant for Christ's sake. Amen.[1]

This same spirit of faithful optimism is found in the words of President Gordon B. Hinckley as he reflected on the challenges of Joseph Smith's time and the problems we face in our own day:

We have every reason to be optimistic. Tragedy is around, yes. Problems everywhere, yes. But look at Nauvoo. Look at what they built here in seven years and then left. But what did they do? Did they lie down and die? No! They went to work! They moved halfway across this continent and turned the soil of a desert and made it blossom as the rose. On that foundation this church has grown into a great worldwide organization affecting for good the lives of people in more than 140 nations. You can't, you don't, build out of pessimism or cynicism. You look with optimism, work with faith, and things happen.[2]

The lives of both the Prophet Joseph Smith and President Gordon B. Hinckley reflect a remarkable resiliency and the ability of all of our prophets, past and present, to follow the Savior's admonition to "be of good cheer" in spite of the many challenges they have faced (Matthew 14:27; see also Matthew 9:2; John 16:33; Acts 23:11; 3 Nephi 1:13; D&C 61:36). It has been said of President Hinckley that his personal motto is "Things will work out. If you keep trying and praying and working, things will work out. They always do."[3] President Hinckley's motto is reminiscent of the Lord's counsel to Joseph Smith in the Doctrine and Covenants, "Search diligently, pray always, and be believing, and all things shall work together for your good, if ye walk uprightly and remember the covenant wherewith ye have covenanted one with another" (D&C 90:24; see also Romans 8:28).

THE FOREKNOWLEDGE OF GOD

One of the prophetic answers that allows us to have hope, confidence, and strength as we deal with the hard questions we have to face in mortality is the doctrine of the "foreknowledge of God" (Alma 13:3; see also Acts 2:23; 1 Peter 1:2). The Book of Mormon prophet Jacob defined the doctrine of the foreknowledge of God and the broader doctrine of His omniscience when he taught, "O how great the holiness of our God! For he knoweth all things, and there is not anything save he knows it" (2 Nephi 9:20). God's foreknowledge is concerned with future events; His omniscience is His complete knowledge of past and present as well as of the future. We can have absolute confidence that the answers God provides to our questions are perfectly reliable, and we can also be assured that His knowledge of the past, present, and future is not simply an educated guess but is complete knowledge. The Prophet Joseph Smith taught:

> Without the knowledge of all things God would not be able to save any portion of his creatures; for it is by reason of the knowledge which he has of all things, from the beginning to the end, that enables him to give that understanding to his creatures by which they are made partakers of eternal life; and if it were not for the idea

existing in the minds of men that God had all knowledge it would be impossible for them to exercise faith in him.[4]

Elder Neal A. Maxwell has observed, "Below the scripture that declares that God knows 'all things' there is no footnote reading 'except that God is a little weak in geophysics'!"[5] Whether the challenges we are facing have to do with geophysics, geopolitics, or any other concern, no matter how large or small, we can have confidence that He from whom we are seeking counsel understands the subject and the situation perfectly and that He wants us to call upon Him.

On November 17, 2001, two football teams, one representing Brigham Young University and the other the University of Utah, played each other in their annual rivalry. Generally when I watch any team play in which I am interested, my heart beats faster, and, strangely enough, my feet perspire at critical junctures. This game, however, was different from any other game I had ever watched between these two long-time opponents. Even though the game was close and several of my students and one of my neighbors were playing for BYU, I watched the game in a state of calm, without any increase in heart rate or additional perspiration. Had I matured beyond caring so much about a simple game? Had I lost my interest in football? No (much to the chagrin of my wife and daughter), I hadn't. The reason for my calm in the midst of the storm of a hotly contested rivalry was that I already knew the outcome. I had been unable to watch the game live, so a friend recorded it on video and took it to my home so I could watch it later that night.

Many battles and wars are yet to be fought in our own lives and in the future of the kingdom of God, conflicts that are much more significant than an athletic contest, but it is important to remember that He cares about anything that concerns us—even a game. It is especially important to know that the eventual outcome of all the problems we are facing is known by God and that good will eventually triumph over evil. The Savior has promised, "He that remaineth steadfast and is not overcome, the same shall be saved" (Joseph Smith–Matthew 1:11). If we are living our lives with Christ as our foundation, we can have absolute confidence that "all things wherewith you have been afflicted shall work together for your good, and to my name's glory, saith the Lord" (D&C 98:3).

In Corrie ten Boom's book *The Hiding Place,* an inspiring account of faith and courage amidst the horrors of World War II, we read these words of wisdom from Corrie's sister, Betsie: "But if God has shown us bad times ahead, it's enough for me that He knows about them. That's why He sometimes shows us things, you know—to tell us that this too is in His hands."[6] The prophet Mormon taught us something similar when he asked latter-day readers of the Book of Mormon, "Know ye not that ye are in the hands of God?" (Mormon 5:23; see also Isaiah 46:9–10). Knowing that God is perfectly aware of the problems we face in the present and are yet to face in the future can comfort us as we seek the solutions to those problems.

Some people are troubled with the seeming paradox that

God knows the future and yet we are still free to make choices. These individuals tend to believe that God's knowledge of what we will do forces us to behave in one way or another. Elder Neal A. Maxwell has offered an important insight:

> Some find the doctrines of the omniscience and fore-knowledge of God troubling because these seem, in some way, to constrict their individual agency. This concern springs out of a failure to distinguish between how it is that God knows with perfection what is to come but that *we* do not know, thus letting a very clear and simple doctrine get obscured by our own finite view of things. . . . Ever to be emphasized, however, is the reality that God's "seeing" is not the same thing as His "causing" something to happen.[7]

My knowledge of the final score of the BYU–University of Utah football game did not in any way influence the outcome of the game. Although it is true that I was looking back on an event that had already occurred, and God's foreknowledge concerns His looking forward to incidents that will yet occur, nonetheless, knowledge of an event does not force nor alter its existence. Elder James E. Talmage taught:

> Many people have been led to regard this foreknowl-edge of God as a predestination whereby souls are designated for glory or condemnation even before their birth in the flesh, and irrespective of individual merit or demerit. This heretical doctrine [predestination] seeks to

rob Deity of mercy, justice, and love; it would make God appear capricious and selfish, directing and creating all things solely for His own glory, caring not for the suffering of His victims. How dreadful, how inconsistent is such an idea of God! It leads to the absurd conclusion that the mere knowledge of coming events must act as a determining influence in bringing about those occurrences. God's knowledge of spiritual and of human nature enables Him to conclude with certainty as to the actions of any of His children under given conditions; yet that knowledge is not of compelling force upon the creature.[8]

The Lord has said that He "knoweth all things, for all things are present" (D&C 38:2) before Him. From this we learn the additional truth that His knowledge and ability to counsel and comfort are possible not simply because He knows us well, can remember what has happened, and can predict what will follow, but—as the Prophet Joseph Smith taught—"the past, the present, and the future were and are, with Him, one eternal 'now.'"[9] Understanding the doctrine of foreknowledge and that God "know[s] the end from the beginning" (Abraham 2:8) can provide us with great comfort and confidence in His ability to direct our lives.

THE DOCTRINE OF OPPOSITION

A profound doctrine that provides us with additional insight and understanding as we face the challenges of mortality is the doctrine of opposition. The familiar phrase from the

prophet Lehi, "For it must needs be, that there is an opposition in all things" (2 Nephi 2:11), reveals a doctrine that is
unique to Latter-day Saint theology. Many religions embrace
the idea that if Adam and Eve had not partaken of the fruit of
the tree of knowledge of good and evil, all mankind would be
living in the Garden of Eden free from pain and any opposition. Lehi clarifies the doctrine by stating, "Adam fell that men
might be; and men are, that they might have joy" (2 Nephi
2:25). Adam and Eve left the garden of Eden, and so must
we—opposition is a part of the Lord's plan for all mankind.

Elder Joseph B. Wirthlin of the Quorum of the Twelve
Apostles has written: "Life was made for struggle; and exaltation, success, and victory were never meant to be cheap or to
come easily. The tides of life often challenge us. To understand
why it has to be this way, we should maintain our understanding, our faith, and our courage by a constant rereading of
Second Nephi, chapter two, the substance of which is set forth
in this excerpt: 'For it must needs be, that there is an opposition in all things' (2 Ne. 2:11)."[10] Elder Wirthlin's counsel and
the instruction given by Lehi to his son Jacob eloquently illustrate the necessity of trials, tribulations, and afflictions in
coming to understand the "nature of happiness" (Alma 41:11).

Opposition generally accompanies progress. Elder Jeffrey R.
Holland has taught that "before great moments, certainly
before great spiritual moments, there can come adversity, opposition, and darkness. Life has some of those moments for us,
and occasionally they come just as we are approaching an
important decision or a significant step in our life."[11] This has

certainly been true in the lives of the prophets of God. The appearance of the Father and the Son to the Prophet Joseph Smith in the Sacred Grove was preceded by the adversary's attempt to destroy him:

> After I had retired to the place where I had previously designed to go, having looked around me, and finding myself alone, I kneeled down and began to offer up the desires of my heart to God. I had scarcely done so, when immediately I was seized upon by some power which entirely overcame me, and had such an astonishing influence over me as to bind my tongue so that I could not speak. Thick darkness gathered around me, and it seemed to me for a time as if I were doomed to sudden destruction.
>
> But, exerting all my powers to call upon God to deliver me out of the power of this enemy which had seized upon me, and at the very moment when I was ready to sink into despair and abandon myself to destruction—not to an imaginary ruin, but to the power of some actual being from the unseen world, who had such marvelous power as I had never before felt in any being—just at this moment of great alarm, I saw a pillar of light exactly over my head, above the brightness of the sun, which descended gradually until it fell upon me.
>
> It no sooner appeared than I found myself delivered from the enemy which held me bound. When the light rested upon me I saw two Personages, whose brightness and glory defy all description, standing above me in the

air. One of them spake unto me, calling me by name and said, pointing to the other—*This is My Beloved Son. Hear Him!* (Joseph Smith History 1:15–17)

Not only does opposition often *precede* revelatory or other significant spiritual experiences, as in the case of the First Vision, Satan and his angels will often oppose us *during* and *after* such experiences as well. Soon after the first missionaries of this dispensation were sent by the Prophet Joseph Smith to England and began to experience success, they had a terrifying experience where evil spirits attempted to destroy them and prevent the many miracles that would follow. After experiencing remarkable success and then returning home from England, Elder Heber C. Kimball asked the Prophet whether or not he and his fellow missionaries had done something wrong to invite such an experience. The Prophet Joseph responded to Elder Kimball's concern by stating:

> No, Brother Heber, . . . at that time you were nigh unto the Lord; there was only a veil between you and Him but you could not see Him. When I heard of it, it gave me great joy, for I knew then that the work of God had taken root in that land. It was this that caused the devil to make a struggle to kill you.[12]

After describing some of his own experiences with the opposition of the evil one, the Prophet taught a principle that has blessed many lives: "The nearer a person approaches the Lord, a greater power will be manifested by the adversary to prevent the accomplishment of His purposes."[13] Elder Kimball assumed (as do many of us) that the devil could not do what he had done if they were living righteously. Although it is true that "the devil has no power over us only as we permit him,"[14] we often give him power through our own ignorance and lack of faith in the superior love and power of God. The Lord has taught, "Light and truth forsake that evil one" (D&C 93:37).

Heber C. Kimball's experience in England and the Prophet Joseph's experience in the Sacred Grove are also our experiences, as each of us is called upon to face opposition in the midst of our search for answers to the questions that challenge us. We can expect and prepare for the influence of the adversary as well as the peace promised by our Heavenly Father as we strive to overcome the opposition in our lives.

THE LORD'S COVENANT OF PEACE

In at least two Christmas devotionals given by the First Presidency, President Gordon B. Hinckley contrasted two poems, the first one by English poet William Ernest Henley (1849–1903) and the second by Elder Orson F. Whitney (1855–1931) of the Quorum of the Twelve Apostles. Written in response to Henley's widely celebrated poem "Invictus," Elder Whitney's poem, "The Soul's Captain," known only to a relatively few Latter-day Saints, contains the key to nothing less than peace in this life and eternal life in the world to come. Following are both remarkable poems, showing clearly their similarities and differences.

INVICTUS

Out of the night that covers me,
Black as the Pit from pole to pole,
I thank whatever gods may be
For my unconquerable soul.

In the fell clutch of circumstance,
I have not winced nor cried aloud:
Under the bludgeonings of chance
My head is bloody, but unbowed.

. . . .

It matters not how strait the gate,
How charged with punishments the scroll,
I am the master of my fate:
I am the captain of my soul.[15]

THE SOUL'S CAPTAIN

Art thou in truth? Then what of him
Who bought thee with his blood?
Who plunged into devouring seas
And snatched thee from the flood?

Who bore for all our fallen race
What none but him could bear.—
The God who died that man might live,
And endless glory share?

Of what avail thy vaunted strength,
Apart from his vast might?
Pray that his Light may pierce the gloom,
That thou mayest see aright.

Men are as bubbles on the wave,
As leaves upon the tree.
Thou, captain of thy soul, forsooth!
Who gave that place to thee?

Free will is thine—free agency,
To wield for right or wrong;
But thou must answer unto him
To whom all souls belong.

Bend to the dust that head "unbowed,"
Small part of Life's great whole!
And see in him, and him alone,
The Captain of thy soul.[16]

William Henley wrote "Invictus" during a twenty-month stay in a hospital in Scotland while recovering from serious health problems. His poem represents his own victory over physical adversity and has inspired many in their battle with difficult times. But in the end, "Invictus" is more expressive of an invitation for humankind to trust in themselves rather than to exercise faith in God.

At some point in our lives, each of us discovers that we, in and of ourselves, do not have strength sufficient to overcome the challenges we face. For some, the unconquerable foe may be an unbalanced life, depression, a troubled marriage, divorce, same-sex attraction, abuse, or war. For others, the Goliath may be another adversity that weighs them down. Ultimately, however, the answer to the various challenges we face is the same—the Lord Jesus Christ. The prophet Helaman pleaded with his sons to remember the necessity of founding their lives on

Christ. He taught them that when, not if, the storms of life came, they would need to have the only foundation that would not fail them:

> And now, my sons, remember, remember that it is upon the rock of our Redeemer, who is Christ, the Son of God, that ye *must* build your foundation; that when the devil shall send forth his mighty winds, yea, his shafts in the whirlwind, yea, when all his hail and his mighty storm shall beat upon you, it shall have no power over you to drag you down to the gulf of misery and endless wo, because of the rock upon which ye are built, which is a sure foundation, a foundation whereon if men build they cannot fall. (Helaman 5:12; italics added)

The Book of Mormon prophet Jacob taught, "Our lives passed away like as it were unto us a dream" (Jacob 7:26). Each of us will live in mortality a relatively short time and will eventually die. We will lose beloved family members to death or perhaps a spouse to divorce during our mortal sojourn. Some among us with superior intellects may one day suffer the ravages of Alzheimer's disease. Others who are now physically strong and vigorous will become weak and frail. Beauty fades, strength diminishes, and minds become less lucid, but there is one thing that remains constant—the love of God and His promise of peace. The prophet Isaiah wrote the words of Jehovah: "For the mountains shall depart, and the hills be removed; but my kindness shall not depart from thee, neither shall the covenant of my peace be removed, saith the Lord that hath mercy on thee" (Isaiah 54:10; see also 3 Nephi 22:10). The Lord continues, addressing those who are "afflicted, tossed with tempest, and not comforted" (Isaiah 54:11) by offering words of tender solace:

> And all thy children shall be taught of the Lord; and great shall be the peace of thy children.
>
> In righteousness shalt thou be established: thou shalt be far from oppression; for thou shalt not fear: and from terror; for it shall not come near thee.
>
> Behold, they shall surely gather together, but not by me: whosoever shall gather together against thee shall fall for thy sake. (Isaiah 54:13–15)

The specific terms of the Lord's "covenant of my peace" (Isaiah 54:10), like all other covenants between God and man, are defined by Him and serve as an invitation for us to receive specific blessings. Nearly every Sabbath day we are privileged to renew the covenants we have made with the Lord when we were baptized. These covenants are represented in the blessings offered on the bread and water during the sacrament service. The blessing on the bread reads:

> O God, the Eternal Father, we ask thee in the name of thy Son, Jesus Christ, to bless and sanctify this bread to the souls of all those who partake of it, that they may eat in remembrance of the body of thy Son, and witness unto thee, O God, the Eternal Father, that they are willing to take upon them the name of thy Son, and always

remember him and keep his commandments which he has given them; that they may always have his Spirit to be with them. Amen. (D&C 20:77)

In addition to describing the promises we make, this sacred prayer also contains a description of our Heavenly Father's promise to us and the central means by which we experience His kindness, peace, and direction—the Holy Ghost. Also known as the Comforter, Guide, Revealer, Sanctifier, Teacher, Sealer, and the Holy Spirit of Promise, the Holy Ghost is God's representative to each of us. In his classic work *Key to the Science of Theology,* Elder Parley P. Pratt described a few of the bounteous blessings bestowed upon us through the power of the Holy Ghost:

> The Gift of the Holy Spirit . . . quickens all the intellectual faculties, increases, enlarges, expands and purifies all the natural passions and affections, and adapts them, by the gift of wisdom, to their lawful use. It inspires, develops, cultivates and matures all the fine-toned sympathies, joys, tastes, kindred feelings and affections of our nature. It inspires virtue, kindness, goodness, tenderness, gentleness and charity. It develops beauty of person, form and features. It tends to health, vigor, animation and social feeling. It develops and invigorates all the faculties of the physical and intellectual man. It strengthens, invigorates and gives tone to the nerves. In short, it is, as it were, marrow to the bone, joy to the heart, light to the eyes, music to the ears, and life to the whole being.[17]

The gift of the Holy Ghost is bestowed upon each of us as we exercise faith in Christ, repent of our sins, are baptized and confirmed (or renew our baptismal covenants through partaking of the sacrament worthily), and willingly receive God's direction. I once heard Elder Henry B. Eyring of the Quorum of the Twelve Apostles describe the following verses as containing the keys to a successful life:

> And the first fruits of repentance is baptism; and baptism cometh by faith unto the fulfilling the commandments; and the fulfilling the commandments bringeth remission of sins;
>
> And the remission of sins bringeth meekness, and lowliness of heart; and because of meekness and lowliness of heart cometh the visitation of the Holy Ghost, which Comforter filleth with hope and perfect love, which love endureth by diligence unto prayer, until the end shall come, when all the saints shall dwell with God. (Moroni 8:25–26)

The scriptures plainly teach that the influence of the Holy Ghost is the central means by which our Father in Heaven and the Lord Jesus Christ "show unto [us] all things what [we] should do" (2 Nephi 32:5). It is also the fundamental way by which the covenant of peace described in scripture is fulfilled.

Several years ago I was asked to travel to southern California to present a lecture to a group of Latter-day Saints. During this trip I had an experience that has served as a reminder to me of the importance of listening to the promptings of the Holy Ghost. Upon arriving safely at the airport, I made my way towards one of the rental car agencies to secure my ground transportation for the few days I would be in town. The person at the counter helped me fill out the necessary paperwork and explained that the car I would be driving was equipped with a "GPS." She explained how the "Global Positioning System" was linked with a satellite overhead that kept track of where my car was in relation to a map of the area and how the GPS could direct me anywhere I wanted to travel. I had heard of GPS technology, but I had never driven a car with such a device. Frankly, I didn't see the need for it during my weekend stay—I could find my way on my own. I soon learned, however, just what a blessing such a system could be.

I left my hotel room with plenty of time to drive to the chapel where I would be speaking. From past experience with driving in southern California, I had learned to give myself enough time to allow for freeway delays, incorrect driving instructions, and so on, but I was soon dismayed to find myself in the middle of a traffic jam. The news report on the radio indicated that there had been a multiple car accident with fatalities and that the freeway was closed indefinitely.

After waiting for nearly forty-five minutes, I realized that I was probably not going to make it on time for my speaking engagement. As I was looking for the phone number of the person to call to notify of my situation, I saw the GPS attached to the dashboard. I pressed the power button and was greeted by a pleasant voice welcoming me to the system and inviting me to enter the address of my destination. After I entered the address of the chapel where I was to speak, the same voice asked me if I wanted to "make the most use of the freeway" or the "least use of the freeway."

Considering the freeway closure, I entered "least use" and the voice then directed me to take the next exit. After a few minutes of wondering how I could even get to the next exit, a highway patrolman signaled that those who wanted to could drive on the shoulder of the freeway and exit. I did so, and for the next thirty minutes I was led from street to street by the "still small voice" of the GPS directing me to my destination.

I had no idea where I was going, but I was soon in the parking lot of the chapel—and only five minutes late to begin my presentation to a patient group of Latter-day Saints. My experience with the Global Positioning System was a powerful reminder to me of just how the Holy Ghost can work in our lives if we will listen and follow the promptings given to us to deliver us from the accidents, disappointments, and detours of life.

CONCLUSION

Can we find peace amidst adversity? The Lord answers this question with a straightforward promise and a challenging insight: "Peace I leave with you, my peace I give unto you: not as the world giveth, give I unto you. Let not your heart be troubled, neither let it be afraid" (John 14:27). Peace is one of the Lord's many promises He has given to us, but it may not be the particular peace we are seeking or expecting—His peace is even greater than we can comprehend.

The story is told of a woman who lived on the coast of Ireland at the turn of the last century. She was very wealthy and also very conservative in how she spent her money. Her neighbors were quite surprised when she became one of the first people in the area to have electricity installed in her home. Several weeks after the electricity had been set up, a meter reader visited her and asked if everything was working properly. After listening to her say how happy she was with the new addition to her home, the meter reader said, "I'm wondering if you can explain something to me. Your meter shows scarcely any usage. Are you using your power?"

"Certainly," she answered. "Each evening when the sun sets, I turn on my lights just long enough to light my candles; then I turn them off."[18] The woman had the power available to her, but she did not use it in the way it was intended to be used.

Could we be making the same mistake with regard to the privilege we have of access to the companionship of the Holy Ghost during times of adversity? President Brigham Young taught that many of us are living "far beneath" the blessings that are available to us:

> There is no doubt, if a person lives according to the revelations given to God's people, he may have the Spirit of the Lord to signify to him His will, and to guide and to direct him in the discharge of his duties, in his temporal as well as his spiritual exercises. I am satisfied, however, that in this respect, we live far beneath our privileges.[19]

As Latter-day Saints we have every reason to "be of good cheer" (John 16:33) because of the blessings of the restored gospel of Jesus Christ. The Savior has come to the earth and once again restored His gospel. He has provided living prophets, who are His special witnesses. Even though we have many weaknesses and face many of the same challenges as do those who are not Latter-day Saints, we have been given much to be grateful for and much to look forward to as we draw nearer to the second coming of the Savior. President Ezra Taft Benson once said:

> As the showdown between good and evil approaches, with its accompanying trials and tribulations, Satan is increasingly striving to overcome the Saints with despair, discouragement, despondency, and depression.
>
> Yet, of all people, we as Latter-day Saints should be the most optimistic and the least pessimistic. For while we know that "peace shall be taken from the earth, and the devil shall have power over his own dominion," we are also assured that "the Lord shall have power over his saints, and shall reign in their midst" (D&C 1:35–36).[20]

The lives and the teachings of all our beloved prophets, ancient and modern, reflect this same optimistic and courageous spirit in the face of all kinds of adversity. Each of them has known the Truth, and the Truth has made them free from doubt, fear, and discouragement. The Prophet Joseph Smith once wrote to his cousin George A. Smith: "Never be discouraged, if I were sunk in the lowest pit of Nova Scotia, with the

Rocky Mountains piled on me, I would hang on, exercise faith, and keep up good courage, and I would come out on top."[21] Another time he wrote:

> Now, what do we hear in the gospel which we have received? A voice of gladness! A voice of mercy from heaven; and a voice of truth out of the earth; glad tidings for the dead; a voice of gladness for the living and the dead; glad tidings of great joy. . . .
>
> Brethren, shall we not go on in so great a cause? Go forward and not backward. Courage, brethren; and on, on to the victory! (D&C 128:19, 22)

As we seek answers to the hard questions we are called upon to deal with, it is our privilege and responsibility to live our lives with the same spirit of hope and optimism as that embodied in the lives and teachings of our beloved prophets. Speaking for other prophets as well as for himself, Jacob recorded:

> For, for this intent have we written these things, that they may know that we knew of Christ, and we had a hope of his glory many hundred years before his coming; and not only we ourselves had a hope of his glory, but also all the holy prophets which were before us. . . .
>
> Wherefore, we search the prophets, and we have many revelations and the spirit of prophecy; and having all these witnesses we obtain a hope, and our faith becometh unshaken, insomuch that we truly can

command in the name of Jesus and the very trees obey us, or the mountains, or the waves of the sea.

Nevertheless, the Lord God showeth us our weakness that we may know that it is by his grace, and his great condescensions unto the children of men, that we have power to do these things. (Jacob 4:4, 6–7)

May the Lord continue to bless each of us as we seek prophetic answers to the hard questions we face as individuals, families, and members of The Church of Jesus Christ of Latter-day Saints.

Notes

Introduction

1. Henry B. Eyring, dedication of Avard T. Fairbanks's statue *The Vision,* October 17, 1997. The statue was placed in the atrium of the Joseph Smith Building, Brigham Young University, Provo, Utah. Elder Eyring's words are on the plaque that is part of the exhibit.

2. Neal A. Maxwell, *All These Things Shall Give Thee Experience* (Salt Lake City: Deseret Book, 1979), 1.

3. Harold B. Lee, Conference Report, October 1970, 152.

4. James E. Faust, "The Great Imitator," *Ensign,* November 1987, 35.

5. Joseph Fielding Smith, Conference Report, April 1917, 59–60.

6. Brigham Young, *Journal of Discourses,* 26 vols. (London: Latter-day Saints' Book Depot, 1854–86), 12:257.

7. Hugh B. Brown, Conference Report, April 1964, 81–82.

8. Wilford Woodruff, *Collected Discourses,* ed. Brian H. Stuy, 5 vols. (Burbank, Calif., and Woodland Hills, Utah: B.H.S. Publishing, 1987–92), 1:214.

9. Joseph Smith, *Teachings of the Prophet Joseph Smith,* sel. Joseph Fielding Smith (Salt Lake City: Deseret Book, 1976), 205.

10. Gordon B. Hinckley, quoted in "Hinckley Completes 8-day Tour," *Church News,* May 24, 1997, 10; Boyd K. Packer, "The Shield of Faith," *Ensign,* May 1995, 8.

11. Harold B. Lee, Conference Report, October 1970, 152.

12. Joseph Smith, *History of The Church of Jesus Christ of Latter-day Saints,* ed. B. H. Roberts, 2d ed. rev., 7 vols. (Salt Lake City: The Church of Jesus Christ of Latter-day Saints, 1932–51), 6:428.

CHAPTER ONE

Self, Family, Church, and Profession: How Can a Proper Balance Be Achieved?

1. Gordon B. Hinckley, "Rejoice in Privilege to Serve," satellite broadcast, June 21, 2003; retrieved 2003; see also *Church News,* June 28, 2003.

2. Richard G. Scott, "First Things First," *Ensign,* May 2001, 7.

3. *http://graceland.gentle.org/bag/chlite.html;* retrieved 2003.

4. Thomas S. Monson, "The Lord's Way," *Ensign,* May 1990, 93.

5. Joseph Smith, *Lectures on Faith,* comp. N. B. Lundwall (Salt Lake City: Deseret Book, 1985), 6:7.

6. Ezra Taft Benson, "The Great Commandment—Love the Lord," *Ensign,* May 1988, 4; emphasis in original.

7. Smith, *Lectures on Faith,* 6:4.

8. Boyd K. Packer, *"That All May Be Edified"* (Salt Lake City: Bookcraft, 1982), 90.

9. W. E. Vine, M. F. Unger, and W. White Jr., *Vine's Complete Expository Dictionary of Old and New Testament Words* (Nashville: Thomas Nelson Publishers, 1996), 140, s.v. "cumber"; 89, s.v. "care, careful."

10. Jeffrey R. Holland and Patricia T. Holland, *On Earth As It Is in Heaven* (Salt Lake City: Deseret Book, 1989), 80–82.

11. Spencer W. Kimball, "The False Gods We Worship," *Ensign,* June 1976, 4.

12. Ibid.; emphasis added.

13. Ibid., 5.

14. Neal A. Maxwell, *Notwithstanding My Weakness* (Salt Lake City: Deseret Book, 1981), 5.

15. Boyd K. Packer, "Covenants," *Ensign,* November 1990, 85.

16. "Know This, That Every Soul Is Free," *Hymns of The Church of Jesus Christ of Latter-day Saints* (Salt Lake City: The Church of Jesus Christ of Latter-day Saints, 1985), no. 240.

17. Harold B. Lee, *The Teachings of Harold B. Lee,* ed. Clyde J. Williams (Salt Lake City: Bookcraft, 1996), 615.

18. C. S. Lewis, *Mere Christianity* (New York: Macmillan, 1960), 161.

19. John A. Widtsoe, *Evidences and Reconciliations,* arr. G. Homer Durham, 3 vols. in 1 (Salt Lake City: Improvement Era, 1960), 194.

CHAPTER TWO

Is Depression a Sin or a Sickness?

1. Troy Goodman, "Utahns No. 1 in Use of Anti-Depressants," *Salt Lake Tribune,* June 21, 2001, A1. See also Cherrill Crosby, "The Ups and Downs of Prozac—Utah's Favorite Drug," *Salt Lake Tribune,* March 27, 1994, A1.

2. Daniel K Judd, "Religiosity, Mental Health, and the Latter-day Saints," in *Latter-day Saint Social Life: Social Research on the LDS Church and Its Members,* ed. James T. Duke (Provo, Utah: Brigham Young University, Religious Studies Center, 1998), 491.

3. Daniel K Judd, "Religious Affiliation and Mental Health," *AMCAP Journal* 12, no. 2 (1986): 80.

4. M. Russell Ballard, "You Have Nothing to Fear from the Journey," *Ensign,* May 1997, 61.

5. Jeffrey R. Holland, "Look to God and Live," *Ensign,* November 1993, 13.

6. Alexander B. Morrison, *Valley of Sorrow: A Layman's Guide to Understanding Mental Illness* (Salt Lake City: Deseret Book, 2003), 50.

7. Boyd K. Packer, *"That All May Be Edified"* (Salt Lake City: Bookcraft, 1982), 94.

8. Adapted from the *Diagnostic and Statistical Manual of Mental Disorders,* 3d ed. (Washington, D.C.: American Psychiatric Association, 1980), 214.

9. Joseph Smith, *Teachings of the Prophet Joseph Smith,* sel. Joseph Fielding Smith (Salt Lake City: Deseret Book, 1976), 364.

10. James E. Talmage, Conference Report, October 1913, 117.

11. Morrison, *Valley of Sorrow,* xv.

12. Boyd K. Packer, "The Touch of the Master's Hand," *Ensign,* May 2001, 23.

13. James E. Faust, "The Gift of the Holy Ghost—A Sure Compass," *Ensign,* April 1996, 5.

14. *Teach Them Correct Principles: A Study in Family Relations* (Salt Lake City: The Church of Jesus Christ of Latter-day Saints, 1987), 7.

15. LDS Bible Dictionary, s.v. "Repentance," 760.

16. Erin Eldridge, *Born That Way? A True Story of Overcoming Same-Sex Attraction with Insights for Friends, Families, and Leaders* (Salt Lake City: Deseret Book, 1994), 87.

17. Neal A. Maxwell, *Glorify Christ* [satellite broadcast, February 2, 2001] (Salt Lake City: The Church of Jesus Christ of Latter-day Saints, 2001), 4.

18. Dallin H. Oaks, "Powerful Ideas," *Ensign,* November 1995, 25.

19. Boyd K. Packer, "The Brilliant Morning of Forgiveness," *Ensign,* November 1995, 20.

20. Brigham Young, *Journal of Discourses,* 26 vols. (London: Latter-day Saints' Book Depot, 1854–86), 4:24.

21. Packer, *"That All May Be Edified,"* 64.

22. Ezra Taft Benson, "Do Not Despair," *Ensign,* October 1986, 2.

23. Neal A. Maxwell, *Things As They Really Are* (Salt Lake City: Bookcraft, 1978), 101–2.

24. Joseph F. Smith, *Gospel Doctrine: Selections from the Sermons and Writings of Joseph F. Smith,* comp. John A. Widtsoe (Salt Lake City: Deseret Book, 1939), 86.

25. Boyd K. Packer, *Let Not Your Heart Be Troubled* (Salt Lake City: Bookcraft, 1991), 51.

26. C. S. Lewis, *Mere Christianity* (New York: Macmillan, 1960), 189.

CHAPTER THREE

"Can Ye Be Angry, and Not Sin?"

1. Burton C. Kelly, "Let All . . . Anger . . . Be Put Away from You: The Case against Anger" [paper presented at the meeting of the Association of Mormon Counselors and Psychotherapists], Salt Lake City, Utah, September 28, 1978.

2. William J. Bennett, "Quantifying America's Decline," *Wall Street Journal,* March 15, 1993.

3. Russell M. Nelson, "The Canker of Contention," *Ensign,* May 1989, 68.

4. Neal A. Maxwell, *Plain and Precious Things* (Salt Lake City: Bookcraft, 1983), 40.

5. John W. Welch, *Illuminating the Sermon at the Temple and Sermon on the Mount* (Provo, Utah: FARMS, 1999), 200.

6. Richard D. Draper to Daniel K Judd.

7. A computer search of the Old Testament revealed that the Hebrew word for anger (*'ap*) appears 455 times, of which 375 times it refers to the anger of the Lord. There are 42 instances of the Lord's anger in the Book of Mormon (out of 150 total instances of a form of the word *anger*).

8. The Greek work for *anger* in this text is *orgē,* which indicates a settled or abiding condition of mind. The other most common Greek word for anger is *thumós,* which indicates a more agitated condition or outburst. *Thumós* is generally translated into English as "wrath."

9. Brigham Young, *Journal of Discourses,* 26 vols. (London: Latter-day Saints' Book Depot, 1854–86), 5:228.

10. David O. McKay, Conference Report, April 1958, 5.

11. Joseph Smith, *Lectures on Faith,* comp. N. B. Lundwall (Salt Lake City: Deseret Book, 1985), 3:4.

12. *Sharpness:* "keen edge or fine point." Noah Webster, *An American Dictionary of the English Language* (New York: S. Converse, 1828; reprint, San Francisco: Foundation of an American Christian Education, 1989), s.v. "sharpness." Instead of meaning an angry outburst, perhaps *sharpness* could mean being specific concerning the communication of differences.

13. C. Terry Warner, *Bonds That Make Us Free: Healing Our Relationships, Coming to Ourselves* (Salt Lake City: Shadow Mountain, 2001), 113–14.

14. Moses 5:18–38; Carol Tavris, *Anger: The Misunderstood Emotion* (New York: Simon and Schuster, 1982).

15. John Bradshaw, "Our Families, Ourselves," *Lear's Magazine,* November-December 1988, 75–76.

16. C. S. Lewis, *Mere Christianity* (New York: Macmillan, 1960), 164–65.

17. Private correspondence with the author; used by permission; also in Daniel K Judd, *The Simpleness of the Way* (Salt Lake City: Bookcraft, 1998), 108–9.

CHAPTER FOUR

Is Divorce the Answer to a Faltering Marriage?

1. First Presidency and the Quorum of the Twelve Apostles, "The Family: A Proclamation to the World," *Ensign,* November 1995, 102.

2. Steven Mintz and Susan Kellogg, *Domestic Revolutions: A Social History of American Family Life* (New York: Free Press, 1988), 206.

3. Ibid., 205–6.

4. Gordon B. Hinckley, "Look to the Future," *Ensign,* November 1997, 69.

5. Tim L. Heaton and Kristen L. Goodman, "Religion and Family Formation," in *Religion, Mental Health, and the Latter-day Saints,* ed. Daniel K Judd (Provo: Brigham Young University, Religious Studies Center, 1999), 122.

6. Ibid.

7. Richard G. Scott, "First Things First," *Ensign,* May 2001, 7.

8. Irving Lehrman, quoted in Michael Gold, "Family: A Spiritual Guide," in *Taking Sides: Clashing Views on Controversial Issues in Religion,* ed. Daniel K Judd (Guilford, Conn.: McGraw-Hill/ Dushkin, 2003), 140. See also Rabbi Gold's website: rabbigold.com.

9. James E. Talmage, *Jesus the Christ* (Salt Lake City: Deseret Book, 1986), 450, for greater detail on the debate between Rabbis Hillel and Shammi.

10. Bruce R. McConkie, *Doctrinal New Testament Commentary,* 3 vols. (Salt Lake City: Bookcraft, 1965–73), 1:547.

11. David O. McKay, *Treasures of Life* (Salt Lake City: Deseret Book, 1965), 66.

12. James E. Faust, "Father, Come Home," *Ensign,* May 1993, 36–37.

13. Gordon B. Hinckley, "What God Hath Joined Together," *Ensign,* May 1991, 74.

14. Joseph Fielding Smith, *Doctrines of Salvation,* 3 vols. (Salt Lake City: Bookcraft, 1954–56), 2:76.

15. Howard W. Hunter, "Reading the Scriptures," *Ensign,* November 1979, 65.

16. Linda J. Waite and Maggie Gallagher, *The Case for Marriage: Why Married People Are Happier, Healthier, and Better Off Financially* (New York: Doubleday, 2000), 149.

17. Paul R. Amato and Alan Booth, *A Generation at Risk: Growing Up in an Era of Upheaval* (Cambridge, Mass.: Harvard University Press, 1997), 238.

18. Joseph Smith, *Teachings of the Prophet Joseph Smith,* sel. Joseph Fielding Smith (Salt Lake City: Deseret Book, 1976), 255–56.

19. Boyd K. Packer, *"That All May Be Edified"* (Salt Lake City: Bookcraft, 1982), 94.

20. Ibid., 291.

21. Waite and Gallagher, *Case for Marriage,* 125.

22. Ibid., 135.

23. Ibid., 136.

24. Hinckley, "Look to the Future," 69.

25. Henry B. Eyring, *Because He First Loved Us* (Salt Lake City: Deseret Book, 2002), ix.

26. *Oxford English Dictionary,* compact ed. (Oxford: Oxford University Press, 1988), s.v. "Atonement."

CHAPTER FIVE

Is Homosexuality a Sin or a Biological Fact?

1. Gordon B. Hinckley, "What Are People Asking about Us?" *Ensign,* November 1998, 70.

2. From a letter in possession of the author. Identifying characteristics have been changed to protect the privacy of the letter writer and his family.

3. Dallin H. Oaks, "Same-Gender Attraction," *Ensign,* October 1995, 9.

4. Robert Spitzer, "Can Some Gay Men and Lesbians Change Their Sexual Orientation? 200 Participants Reporting a Change from

Homosexual to Heterosexual Orientation," *Archives of Sexual Behavior* 32, no. 5 (October 2003): 403.

5. Warren Throckmorten, "Initial Empirical and Clinical Findings Concerning the Change Process for Ex-Gays," *Professional Psychology: Research and Practice* 33, no. 3 (June 2002): 242–48; A. Dean Byrd and Stony Olson, "Homosexuality: Innate and Immutable?" *Regent University Law Review* 14, no. 2 (2001–02): 512–53.

6. *Understanding and Helping Those Who Have Homosexual Problems* (Salt Lake City: The Church of Jesus Christ of Latter-day Saints, 1992), 3–4.

7. Erin Eldridge, *Born That Way? A True Story of Overcoming Same-Sex Attraction with Insights for Friends, Families, and Leaders* (Salt Lake City: Deseret Book, 1994), 121.

8. *Oxford English Dictionary,* compact ed. (Oxford: Oxford University Press, 1988), s.v. "Religion."

9. Ezra Taft Benson, "Mighty Change of Heart," *Ensign,* October 1989, 2–5; emphasis added.

10. Joseph Smith, *Journal of Discourses,* 26 vols. (London: Latter-day Saints' Book Depot, 1854–86), 6:4–5.

11. Gordon B. Hinckley, "Reverence and Morality," *Ensign,* May 1987, 47.

12. *Understanding and Helping Those Who Have Homosexual Problems,* 1.

13. Oaks, "Same-Gender Attraction," 9.

14. First Presidency, "Standards of Morality and Fidelity," November 14, 1991; in possession of the author.

15. Ibid.

16. Boyd K. Packer, *The Great Plan of Happiness* [address to religious educators] (Salt Lake City: The Church of Jesus Christ of Latter-day Saints, 1993), 3.

17. Neal A. Maxwell, "Thanks Be to God," *Ensign,* July 1982, 51.

18. Bruce R. McConkie, *A New Witness for the Articles of Faith* (Salt Lake City: Deseret Book, 1985), 81.

19. First Presidency and the Quorum of the Twelve Apostles, "The Family: A Proclamation to the World," *Ensign,* November 1995, 102.

20. Harold B. Lee, *The Teachings of Harold B. Lee,* ed. Clyde J. Williams (Salt Lake City: Bookcraft, 1996), 232.

21. Joseph Smith, *Teachings of the Prophet Joseph Smith,* sel. Joseph Fielding Smith (Salt Lake City: Deseret Book, 1976), 343.

22. Spencer W. Kimball, *Faith Precedes the Miracle* (Salt Lake City: Deseret Book, 1972), 97.

23. Eldridge, *Born That Way?* 127.

24. Richard G. Scott, "True Friends That Lift," *Ensign,* November 1988, 77.

25. Boyd K. Packer, "The Brilliant Morning of Forgiveness," *Ensign,* November 1995, 20.

26. Neal A. Maxwell, "According to the Desire of Our Hearts," *Ensign,* November 1996, 21.

CHAPTER SIX

Can a Person Who Has Been Abused Be Healed?

1. John Taylor, *Journal of Discourses,* 26 vols. (London: Latter-day Saints' Book Depot, 1854–86), 7:199.

2. Merrill J. Bateman, "The Power to Heal from Within," *Ensign,* May 1995, 4.

3. Merrill J. Bateman, "A Peculiar Treasure," *Brigham Young University 1996–97 Speeches* (Provo, Utah: Brigham Young University, 1997), 10.

4. *Responding to Abuse: Helps for Ecclesiastical Leaders* (Salt Lake City: The Church of Jesus Christ of Latter-day Saints, 1995), 1.

5. Gordon B. Hinckley, "Save the Children," *Ensign,* November 1994, 54.

6. Thomas S. Monson, "Precious Children—a Gift from God," *Ensign,* November 1991, 69.

7. James Strong, *The Exhaustive Concordance of the Bible,* electronic ed. (Ontario: Woodside Bible Fellowship, 1996), s.v. "Offend."

8. Carlfred Broderick, *My Parents Married on a Dare* (Salt Lake City: Deseret Book, 1996), 88.

9. Ibid., 89.

10. Gordon B. Hinckley, "I Believe," *Ensign,* August 1992, 6.

11. Carlfred Broderick, *One Flesh, One Heart: Putting Celestial Love into Your Temple Marriage* (Salt Lake City: Deseret Book, 1986), 31–32.

12. First Presidency and the Quorum of the Twelve Apostles, "The Family: A Proclamation to the World," *Ensign,* November 1995, 102.

13. Richard G. Scott, "Receive the Temple Blessings," *Ensign,* May 1999, 26.

14. Gordon B. Hinckley, "Women of the Church," *Ensign,* November 1996, 68.

15. First Presidency and the Quorum of the Twelve Apostles, "The Family: A Proclamation to the World," 102.

16. Boyd K. Packer, *"That All May Be Edified"* (Salt Lake City: Bookcraft, 1982), 139.

17. Gordon B. Hinckley, "The Healing Power of Christ," *Ensign,* November 1988, 59.

18. Letter from the First Presidency, February 7, 1985, quoted in "Hidden Agony," *New Era,* March 1992, 44.

19. Richard G. Scott, "Healing the Tragic Scars of Abuse," *Ensign,* May 1992, 32.

20. Anonymous, "The Journey to Healing," *Ensign,* September 1997, 21.

21. Scott, "Healing the Tragic Scars of Abuse," 32.

22. Anonymous, "Journey to Healing," 19.

23. Anonymous, "My Journey to Forgiving," *Ensign,* February 1997, 43.

24. Joseph Fielding Smith, *Doctrines of Salvation,* comp. Bruce R. McConkie, 3 vols. (Salt Lake City: Bookcraft, 1954–56), 1:61.

25. Harold B. Lee, *Stand Ye in Holy Places* (Salt Lake City: Deseret Book, 1974), 186.

26. Dallin H. Oaks, *The Lord's Way* (Salt Lake City: Deseret Book, 1991), 173–74.

CHAPTER SEVEN

Is It Possible to Reconcile War with the Teachings of Christ?

1. David O. McKay, Conference Report, April 1942, 70–71.

2. Ibid., 71–72.

3. Harold B. Lee, Conference Report, October 1970, 152.

4. C. S. Lewis, *God in the Dock,* ed. Walter Hooper (Grand Rapids, Mich.: Eerdmans, 1970), 294.

5. Ezra Taft Benson, *The Teachings of Ezra Taft Benson* (Salt Lake City: Bookcraft, 1988), 8; emphasis added.

6. Bruce R. McConkie, "Stand Independent above All Other Creatures," *Ensign,* May 1979, 93.

7. Joseph Fielding Smith, Conference Report, April 1937, 59.

8. Gordon B. Hinckley, "War and Peace," *Ensign,* May 2003, 80.

9. Ezra Taft Benson, *A Witness and a Warning: A Modern-Day Prophet Testifies of the Book of Mormon* (Salt Lake City: Deseret Book, 1988), 21.

10. Lee Davidson, "Bush Holds Hour Long Prayer Meeting with America's Religious Leaders," *Deseret News,* September 20, 2001.

11. Henry B. Eyring, "Finding Safety in Counsel," *Ensign,* May 1997, 25.

12. Gordon B. Hinckley, "The Times in Which We Live," *Ensign,* November 2001, 74.

13. Gordon B. Hinckley, "The Healing Power of Christ," *Ensign,* November 1988, 54.

14. Joseph Smith, quoted in Spencer W. Kimball, *The Teachings of Spencer W. Kimball,* ed. Edward L. Kimball (Salt Lake City: Bookcraft, 1982), 192.

15. First Presidency and the Quorum of the Twelve Apostles, "The Family: A Proclamation to the World," *Ensign,* November 1995, 102.

16. Joseph Smith, *Teachings of the Prophet Joseph Smith,* sel. Joseph Fielding Smith (Salt Lake City: Deseret Book, 1976), 256.

17. Dallin H. Oaks, *The Lord's Way* (Salt Lake City: Deseret Book, 1991), 143.

CHAPTER EIGHT

Can We Find Peace amidst Adversity?

1. Joseph Smith, *History of The Church of Jesus Christ of Latter-day Saints,* ed. B. H. Roberts, 2d ed. rev., 7 vols. (Salt Lake City: The Church of Jesus Christ of Latter-day Saints, 1932–51), 2:352–53.

2. *New York Times* interview, 1995, as cited in Gordon B. Hinckley, *Teachings of Gordon B. Hinckley* (Salt Lake City: Deseret Book, 1997), 412.

3. Sheri L. Dew, *Go Forward with Faith: The Biography of Gordon B. Hinckley* (Salt Lake City: Deseret Book, 1996), 423.

4. Joseph Smith, *Lectures on Faith,* comp. N. B. Lundwall (Salt Lake City: Deseret Book, 1985), 51–52.

5. Neal A. Maxwell, *All These Things Shall Give Thee Experience* (Salt Lake City: Deseret Book, 1979), 7.

6. Corrie ten Boom, *The Hiding Place* (New York: Bantam Books, 1971), 63.

7. Maxwell, *All These Things,* 20.

8. James E. Talmage, *Articles of Faith* (Salt Lake City: The Church of Jesus Christ of Latter-day Saints, 1973), 191.

9. Smith, *History of the Church,* 4:597.

10. Joseph B. Wirthlin, "Dikes versus Living Water," *Ensign,* November 1976, 28.

11. Jeffrey R. Holland, "Cast Not Away Therefore Your Confidence," Brigham Young University devotional address, March 2, 1999, http://speeches.byu.edu/devo/98-99/HollandW99.html.

12. Orson F. Whitney, *The Life of Heber C. Kimball* (Salt Lake City: Bookcraft, 1992), 131–32.

13. Ibid., 132.

14. Joseph Smith, *Teachings of the Prophet Joseph Smith,* sel. Joseph Fielding Smith (Salt Lake City: Deseret Book, 1976), 181.

15. William Henley, "Invictus," *Oxford Dictionary of Quotations,* 332, as cited in James E. Faust, "The Power of Self-Mastery," *Ensign,* May 2000, 45.

16. Orson F. Whitney, "The Soul's Captain," *Improvement Era,* May 1926, 7.

17. Parley P. Pratt, *Key to the Science of Theology* (Salt Lake City: George Q. Cannon & Sons, 1891), 101–2.

18. David Jeremiah, *The God of the Impossible* [audiotape], cited in Max Lucado, *Just like Jesus* (Nashville: Word Publishing, 1998), 8.

19. Brigham Young, *Journal of Discourses* (London: Latter-day Saints' Book Depot, 1854–86), 12:104.

20. Ezra Taft Benson, *The Teachings of Ezra Taft Benson* (Salt Lake City: Bookcraft, 1988), 401.

21. George A. Smith, *Memoirs of George A. Smith,* 81–82, as cited in John Henry Evans, *An American Prophet,* Classics in Mormon Literature ed. (Salt Lake City: Deseret Book, 1989), 9.

Index

and sin, 62; importance of, 63;
and healing, 70–71
Health, spiritual, 52–54, 61–62,
70–71
Heart, change of, 129–30
Heavenly Father. *See* God
Helaman, 114–15, 229
Henley, William Ernest, 227–29
Hiding Place, The, 221
Hinckley, Gordon B.: on modern
day, 9; on trusting in the Lord,
13–14; on family, 101–2, 120;
on divorce, 109; on abuse,
157, 168–69; on marriage,
163; and priesthood keys,
165–66; on healing power of
Christ, 171, 202–3; on war,
194–95; and George W. Bush,
198; on personal righteousness,
202; on optimism, 218;
contrasts poems, 227
Holland, Jeffrey R., 43, 224
Holland, Patricia T., 25–27
Holy Ghost: testimony of, 8–9;
empowers, 27; loss of, 35, 213;
and teaching, 36, 149–50;
gives peace, 54–55; obeying
promptings of, 94–95, 234;
helps in service, 121; helps
marriages, 122; and healing
from abuse, 177, 180; living
worthily of, 202; helps in
decisions, 206; as God's
promise to us, 232–33;
blessings of, 232, 236
Homosexuality: Gordon B.
Hinckley on, 123–24, 133;
questions about, 124; and
families, 124–26; and
predisposition, 126–27; and
change, 127–28, 131–34;
definition of, 134–38; in

scripture, 136–37; and
behavior, 137–38; as challenge,
145; deliverance from, 148–51
Hope, 215
Humility, 180
Husbands, 109, 159, 162–69

"I Am a Child of God," 58
Idolatry, 28–32, 81, 116
Individualism, 101–2
Inspiration, 6
Integrity, 109
Intent, 196–97
"Invictus," 227–29
Israel, children of, 203–4

Jacob, 159, 183–84, 219, 238
Jefferson, Thomas, 73
Jeremiah, 161
Jesus Christ: and sacrifice, 17; on
priorities, 18; visits Mary and
Martha, 23–24; and balance,
39; perfection of, 56–57;
depression and, 67–71;
righteousness of, 69–70; on
anger, 75–79, 207–8; anger of,
79–82; love of, 80–81; cleanses
temple, 82–86; becoming like,
88, 132, 142–43; and divorce,
105–6; healing power of, 111,
121, 171, 186, 202–3; as
foundation, 112, 114–15, 221,
230; taking name of, 122;
characteristics of, 134, 142; our
need for, 146; and deliverance,
148–51; identifies himself,
152; suffers abuse, 152–56;
sorrow of, 153; on revenge,
177, 206–9, 211; on defiling,
177; on service, 183; and
justice, 191–92; second
coming of, 193; and war,

Medication, 40–41, 53, 60, 171
Mercy, 80, 179, 192, 210
Millennium, 193
Miracles, 154
Missionaries, 214
Money, 29
Monson, Thomas S., 158
Morality, 137–38
Morianton, 174–75
Mormon, 92, 120, 173, 221
Moroni, 79, 195
Moroni, Captain, 196–97, 201
Morrison, Alexander B., 53
Mortality, 117
Moses, 19–23, 106, 203–4
Mosiah, 5–6
Murder, 205–6
Music, 63

Natural man, 3, 99
Neighbors, 18–19
Nelson, Russell M., 73–74
Nephi: on trusting God, 6; on
  Holy Ghost, 9; on Israelites,
  64; on plain and precious parts
  of gospel, 74; on anger, 95–96;
  as strength for Jacob, 183; and
  war, 195–96; obtains plates of
  brass, 199–200
Nephites, 196–98
New Testament, 130–31, 206–13

Oaks, Dallin H.: on self-worth,
  58; on lifestyle, 127; on
  homosexuality, 135; on
  forgiveness, 184; on "resist not
  evil," 207
Obedience, 199–202, 206
Offend, 158–59
Old Testament, 203–6
Opposition: Lehi on, 31, 116–18;
  Spencer W. Kimball on,

144–45; in Garden of Eden,
  145–46; Joseph Smith and,
  216; doctrine of, 223–27
Optimism, 215–18, 237–39
Organization, 35–36

Packer, Boyd K.: on spiritual
  dependence, 22; on virtues, 32;
  on disappointment, 46; on
  depression, 54; on guilt, 59,
  65–66; on spiritual disorders,
  62; on life as challenge, 117;
  on troubled marriage, 118; on
  plan of salvation, 139–40; on
  repentance, 147–48; on
  marriage, 163–64; on miracles,
  169–70
Pahoran, 208–9
Pain, 155
Parenting, 139
Paul: on natural man, 3; on
  doctrinal differences, 11; on
  pleasure, 31; on temptation,
  37–38; on godly sorrow, 66; on
  marriage, 109; on "thorn in the
  flesh," 134; on homosexuality,
  136, 147; on revenge, 210; on
  civil and religious leaders, 212
Peace, 191–94, 214, 215–16,
  227–35
Peacemakers, 214
Peninnah, 48–49
People, voice of, 5–6
Perfection, 55–57
Pessimism, 218
Peter, 7, 211
Pharaoh, 203
Philosophies, of world, 4–6
Pioneers, 41–42, 145
Plan of salvation, 139–41, 154–55
Pleasure, 31
Politics, 190–91